The Essential Doctrines of Christianity

A Guidebook for the Life of Faith

By Rev. Dr. Abraham Chang-wan Hahn

The Essential Doctrines of Christianity

A Guidebook for the Life of Faith

By Rev. Dr. Abraham Chang-wan Hahn

Translated by Rev. Jacob Do-hong Choi, D.Min.
Written by Rev and Dr. Abrahm Chanwan Hahn
D.Min in Miss. from Midwest University

Former professor for Chicago Presbyterian Theological Seminary

Former moderator of the Central Presbytery of Korean Presbyterian Church Abroad

Former president of the Korean Church Federation of Greater Chicago

Former president of the presidents' association for Korean Churches in Chicago

Former senior/emeritus pastor of YoungNak Presbyterian Church in Chicago

Translator Profile
Do-hyong Choi, D.Min.
Graduated from Inha University, Korea
Graduated from Full Gospel Theological Seminary, Korea
Graduated from Seoul Theological University, Korea
Graduated from San Francisco Theological Seminary, U.S.A.
A freelance translator and interpreter (translated about 40 books)
Pastor, Evangelical Holiness Church of Love in Korea

Special thanks goes to my Project Team at Createspace, an Amazon.com company, for helping me complete my humble book.

Scripture text, unless otherwise noted, is taken from the King James (Authorized) Version of the Bible.

ISBN: 0615504337
ISBN-13: 9780615504339

Contents

Foreword by Rev. Ji-il Bang (Former Chairman of the Presbyterian Church Meeting) 1
Author's Preface. 3
Chapter 1 The Way to Salvation .7
    Three Temporal Steps of Salvation 17
Chapter 2 The Goal of a Christian Life 21
    The Kingdom of God and the
    Kingdom of Heaven 23
    The Righteousness of God 24
    How to Glorify God 25
    The Works of God 26
    Benediction 27
    Conditions for Going with the Lord 29
    Born Again 32
    Conclusion 42
Chapter 3 Doctrine of Man 45
    The Theory of Evolution 47
    The Trinity 65
    The Doctrine of God 79
    Creationism 90
    Dichotomy and Trichotomy. 108
    Eleven Places after the Death of Human Beings . . . 111
    The Mark of the Beast 126
    Eschatology 131
    Suicide 142
    Conflicts in the Church 144
    Conclusion 157
Appendix 1 Hardships 159
Appendix 2 Prayers Answered. 169
Appendix 3 A History of the Bible 175

Foreword

Today, there are numerous Christian books, but there are few guidebooks for the life of faith. They are necessary and appropriate for Christian believers. This guidebook should be read by each and every Christian. Because nowadays many people ignore the realities of Christian life, even already saved believers should read this guidebook, so that they may reconfirm their own faith. I recommend this book for building up the faith of every believer.

Rev. Ji-il Bang
Missionary to China
Former Chairman of the General Assembly of the Presbyterian Church in Korea

Author's Preface

The Bible is our only authority because it is inspired by God, and the Holy Spirit has gathered its contents so that the man or woman of God may be perfect and thoroughly equipped for all good works. The Bible establishes correct theology and faith. It is the source through which various problems of the Christian life are to be interpreted and resolved.

Christians must be born again, but this rebirth cannot be accomplished through character improvement based on moral training and discipline, nor through contemplation or awakening through human effort. People can be newly changed and reborn only through the seed of God (1 Pet. 1:23), which shall be planted and grown in us. That is why the Christian life may be called a born again life. In this kind of life, the Holy Spirit, the Spirit of Christ, dwells in us at all times. The life of faith gushes like a spring. It is not a heavy burden to be borne unwillingly, but the Holy Spirit with His infinite power walks always with reborn Christians and transforms them so that they may accomplish a life of love incessantly flowing up like a spring.

With God's help, I have completed this small book, for which I give God heartfelt gratitude so much.

I also extend my thanks to Rev. Ji-il Bang, my beloved teacher, and to Elder Hyeong-gyu Yi, of Qumran Publishing, which published this book in Korean and to Elder Paul Hahn who helped its English version get published.

I sincerely hope and pray that all the readers of this book praise and glorify the Lord God our Father.

Chang-wan Hahn
Aurora, Ill, USA

"I am the way, the truth, and the life: no man cometh unto the Father, but by me" (John 14:6).

(1) Why is Christianity the only religion in which salvation can be found?
(2) Why is Jesus the only Savior?
(3) Why must we believe in Jesus to be saved?

In order to spread the gospel and evangelize the world today, believers must have answers to these three questions. What does the Bible say?

CHAPTER 1

The Way to Salvation

The purpose for us to believe in Jesus is not to be blessed by God with prosperity and success. Of course, because of God's remarkable love and grace, believers may in fact be blessed with a prosperous and successful life. Nevertheless, that is not the purpose of our believing in Jesus. First Peter 1:9 says that the purpose of our faith is the salvation of our souls. Romans 6:22 also says, "But now being made free from sin, and become servants to God, ye have your fruit unto holiness, and the end everlasting life." The primary purpose of our believing in Jesus, then, is to be graced with everlasting life after death. In other words, to not go to permanent hell but to heaven, where we will enjoy an everlasting life.

Christianity is different from the major religions of the world in many ways. (The five major religions of the world are considered to be Christianity, Islam, Buddhism, Confucianism, and Hinduism.) One of the ways in which Christianity differs is regarding sin.

Who goes to heaven and who goes to hell, according to Christianity? One goes to hell or heaven because of his or her sin. Christianity is fundamentally different from the other major religions because it teaches that sinners shall go to hell and sinless people to heaven (see Luke 1:77). According to the teachings of Christianity, *sin* (אטח in Hebrew) means "missing the target," as meant by the Greek word ἁμαρτανω (see Judges 20:16), i.e., missing the word (will) of God.

In the Bible, there are two kinds of commandments: do it and do it not. Not obeying the commandments is a sin. Doing what is prohibited or omitting what is required is also sin (see James 4:17). Not loving our neighbors is a sin because we are commanded to "love your neighbors." Lying is a sin because we are commanded to "not tell a lie." It is a sin to take from "the fruit of the tree of knowledge." Disobeying the word of God is a sin (see James 4:17). The Bible says, "The wages of sin is death" (Rom. 6:23) and "The soul that sinneth, it shall die" (Ezek. 18:4). Romans 5:12 says, "Wherefore, as by one man sin entered into the world, and death by sin; and so death passed upon all men, for that all have sinned." An everlasting life (salvation) is determined based on lack of sin. God's remuneration (reward) is determined according to how one has led his or her life regardless of his or her sins.

In these latter days, what is predominant is secularism, from which comes religious pluralism. This pluralism leads to religious syncretism, which contends that all the religions in the world are the same, which further leads to the theory of religious unification, which asserts that none of the world's religions are perfect and that the strengths of each should be combined and unified into a new world religion that is better than any of the original faiths individually. As a result, a world unified religion that advocates that men have invented their own god in their own imagination according to their image has emerged. In actuality, it is not a religion but a sort of religious philosophy similar to man-made moralism; it is an artificial religion. It is symbolic of the cyborg (cybernetic organism) and the humanoid that will be revealed at the end of the last days. That is why Christian theology today is becoming merely a moral system.

It is possible and sometimes necessary that Christians should dialogue and cooperate with other religions. For example, aid of 150,00 tons of rice from Christians and 50,000 tons from Buddhists can be sent to North Korea, which is suffering from starvation. In this case, the aid need not be transported in separate ships but can be sent in the same ship. Such a trend might be called a theology of commensalism.

However, there are other cases in which Christianity can never concede to Buddhism. The doctrine that only Jesus Christ is our Savior and Christianity is the only religion for acquiring salvation is one example. Religious pluralists and syncretists often say that there is one truth or salvation but that different religions suggest different ways to the same everlasting life. Each religion has a way to salvation in the same way that each mountain road leads to the same peak. This seems to be plausible, but Christianity teaches that men shall not go up a mountain but go across a bridge over an abyss. The bridge is the only way to cross the deep river; there is no other. This teaching is totally different from that of the other religions.

There are numerous kinds of sin in the world: murder, robbery, theft, and pride, as well as civil, religious and moral wrongdoing. All these transgressions are generally grouped into two kinds: original sin and actual sins. The first was committed by Adam and Eve when they ate the fruit of the tree of knowledge. This sin has been inherited from Adam to his offspring and all human beings (Rom. 5:12). Original sin refers to an invisible intrinsic sin; the forbidden fruit was eaten by Adam, not by us.

However, we also have the original sin because we came to have a sinful nature when Adam committed the original sin. The Bible says, "Nevertheless death reigned from Adam

to Moses, even over them that had not sinned after the simili-
tude of Adam's transgression," (Rom. 5:14) which means that
since Adam ate the fruit of the tree of knowledge, we, his offspring, came to have a conscience seared with a hot iron that
cannot sense the guiltiness of sins. So even though we have not
committed demonstrated sins nor eaten the fruit of the tree of
knowledge, we are also inclined to sinning due to Adam's sin
in the same way that bad copies are reproduced when a bad
original is used or the children of slaves are also slaves generation after generation. As the Bible says, "Wherefore, as by one
man sin entered into the world, and death by sin; and so death
passed upon all men, for that all have sinned" (Rom. 5:12),
"Behold, I was shaped in iniquity; and in sin did my mother
conceive me" (Ps. 51:5) and "For I knew that thou wouldest
deal very treacherously, and wast called a transgressor from the
womb" (Isa. 48:8).

Actual or intentional sins are committed willfully. They include not only violent crimes and theft but also sins committed
in the mind, such as curses and rages.

There are no humans who have not committed original and
actual sins. As the Bible says, "All have sinned, and come short
of the glory of God" (Rom. 3:23), and "We have before proved
both Jews and Gentiles, that they are all under sin" (Rom. 3:9).
Can we be saved by leading a righteous life, through our human
actions? To this question, the Bible answers, "By the deeds of
the law there shall no flesh be justified in his sight" (Rom. 3:20),
and "We conclude that a man is justified by faith without the
deeds of the law" (Rom. 3:28). Why is it? According to the Bible,
a sinner is not sentenced to ten-year twenty-year imprisonment
depending upon the weight of their sin; the sinner is sentenced
to the death penalty (see Rom. 6:23, 5:12) no matter how seri-
ous the sin. Because of this, no good deed, no human action can

bring salvation. Anyhow, it is not God's will to drive any person to hell when he or she commits a sin, because God created that person (Gen. 1:27) from the dust of the ground (Gen. 2:7).

Far be it! God has provided us with the only and unique way to be forgiven our sins. The way is described in Leviticus 17:11: "For the life of a creature is in the blood, and I have given it to you to make atonement for yourselves on the altar; it is the blood that makes atonement for one's life." Hebrews 9:22 says, "Without the shedding of blood there is no forgiveness." Other biblical passages speak to the same effect: "The blood of Jesus, his Son, purifies us from all sin" (1 John 1:7). "Since we have now been justified by his blood" (Rom. 5:9). "In whom we have redemption, the forgiveness of sins" (Col. 1:14).

In the Old Testament age, a calf, lamb, or young pigeon was offered as a sin offering. Especially once a year, on the Day of Atonement (מירופיכה-םוי, ידה םוי in Hebrew), the high priest would enter the most holy place, where he would offer a sin offering to remit the sin of the people (see Lev. 16:34; Heb. 9:7). This remittance (forgiveness) of sins is one of the ways that Christianity is fundamentally different from the other religions. In other religions, compensation had to be made to forgive a sin. For example, if one has stolen a quantity of rice, he or she must pay back ten times as much as was stolen to find salvation. In contrast, in Christianity, without shedding blood there is no forgiveness of sins no matter how much compensation is made. In the Old Testament, not only a sin offering was made but an indemnity was made according to the ordinances prescribed by the priests. Yet, this forgiveness given for the blood of beasts is not complete (Heb. 10:4). When we tell a lie ten times a day, it would be a difficult thing to offer a young pigeon as a sin offering ten times a day. It is also really hard for men to present beasts as a ransom whenever they commit a sin.

Nevertheless, the blood of God's only begotten son, Jesus Christ, that flowed when He was crucified was a sin offering made once and for all to pardon all sins past, present and future (Eph. 1:7; Heb. 9:12, 26, 28; Heb. 10:10; Rom. 6:10; 1 Pet. 3:18; Jer. 31:34). Jesus "needeth not daily, as those high priests, to offer up sacrifice, first for his own sins, and then for the people's: for this he did once, when he offered up himself" (Heb. 7:27, 9:25-26). When Jesus was hanged on the cross, the veil of the temple was rent in the midst. (Luke 23:45). The veil is His flesh (Heb. 10:20). That is to say, what was put as a block between men and God has been removed. It implies that Jesus as a mediator (1 Tim. 2:5) has set up a bridge so that men may communicate freely with God. For perfect remittance of our sins, God has sent his only begotten son to earth. Unlike men, God is a spiritual being (John 4:24; 2 Cor. 3:17) and with whom is no variableness, neither shadow of turning (Jam. 1:17). His only begotten son is also a spiritual being without blood and flesh. A spiritual being, which cannot bleed or die cannot make any difference on the earth in connection with forgiveness of sins, even though he is God's son. In order to redeem human beings, a being with human body and blood had to come down and die on earth. That is why about two thousand years ago Jesus was born in human flesh from the Virgin Mary at Bethlehem in Judea (Matt. 1:16). This incident is commonly called the incarnation, which means that spiritual Son of God has come in human flesh (Rom. 1:4; Matt. 27:54; Mark 15:39; 1 Tim. 1:15). God's son, who resides in unchangeable eternity, came down to the changeable limited time frame of this world.

When I was a schoolboy, if I said that the Virgin Mary gave birth to Jesus I would be asked, "Are you stupid or something? Don't you know about biology? How can a virgin bear a child? Don't you know that man is composed of forty-six chromosomes, including the XX chromosome that leads to a daughter and XY chromosome that leads to a son?"

I could not given an answer to these questions but would mutter to myself, "It is very strange. The Bible really says the Virgin Mary had borne Jesus."

Anyhow, years ago, a twenty-year-old German virgin called Mary actually bore a child who is Korean. How? The child was a test tube baby borne by a surrogate mother. The virgin produced the child through test tube insemination executed between a Korean man living in America and a Korean woman living in Korea. This kind of even now routine.

In 1978, the first-ever test tube baby was produced in the world. The test-tube baby named Louise Brown, was naturally borne by Mrs. Lesley Brown by means of in vitro fertilization, an artificial insemination method developed by two British doctors, Robert Edwards and Patrick Steptoe. An estimated four million babies have been conceived using this method. In February 1996, a lamb was clones in Scotland by Ian Wilmut of Roslin Institute. The lamb was administered euthanasia in 2003 after it contracted a lung disease. Today, it is not unusual or unscientific to hear people talk about human cloning.

In the twenty-first century then, it can not be nonsense to say the Virgin Mary gave birth to Jesus. Furthermore, I believe that one day in the future we will see another Mary giving birth to another Jesus.

In chapter 1 of Luke's Gospel, the angel Gabriel said to Virgin Mary, "Behold, thou shalt conceive in thy womb, and bring forth a son, and shalt call his name JESUS" (1:31), who will save his people from their sins. At this, Mary retorted, "How shall this be, seeing I know not a man?" (verse 34). Then, the angel said, "With God nothing shall be impossible" (verse 37), meaning that Jesus conceived in her is of the Holy Ghost.

So Jesus was conceived of the Holy Ghost in the Virgin Mary. He does not have the original sin inherited from Adam and has known no sin (2 Cor. 5:21; Heb. 4:15; 1 Pet. 2:22).

Why does only Jesus not have the original sin? Isn't it clearly said in the Bible that Jesus was conceived in the Virgin Mary, who was a human being having the original sin? Jesus does not have the original sin because the original sin is inherited through man (Adam) only, not through woman (Eve) (Rom. 5:12). It is commonly said that man is a seed while woman is a field. This saying implies that what a field produces is determined not by the field itself but by the seed (i.e., bean or red-bean) (Gal. 6:7). The Bible clearly says that Jesus was conceived of the Holy Spirit, which does not have the original sin or a sinful nature (Matt. 1:18, 20; Luke 1:35; Isa. 7:14). The Virgin Mary simply served as a surrogate mother (as in the case of a test tube baby) and the original sin, which is inherited by human beings, has not been passed to Him.

Why can only Jesus save human beings from sin? This is theologically very important. There are numberless people in the world who have sacrificed and died for others. In ancient days, a virgin or child was often sacrificed for others. Why did not they save human beings from sin?

It is because they all had the original sin and a sinful human nature, which is not adequate for a perfect sacrifice. In contrast, Jesus came to this earth without original sin and was conceived sinless of the Holy Spirit (Isa. 7:14 and Luke 1:35). Therefore, Jesus came as the Lamb of God, which takes away the sin of the world (John 1:29). When Jesus was resurrected, it was proof that only Jesus has redeemed all human beings from sin. Without His resurrection, it would be of no avail that Jesus was crucified to save us. The Bible says, "If Christ be not raised, your faith is vain; ye are yet in your sins" (1 Cor. 15:17).

No human being has ever broken the power of death except for Jesus Christ, who was resurrected in order to redeem all human beings from sin. About two thousand year ago, this Jesus was bleeding on the cross to remit the sins of all human beings past, present, and future. It is called a sacrificial salvation (Gal. 1:4; Luke 1:77-78; 2 Cor. 5:21; Rom. 4:25; 1 Pet. 2:24; John 1:29). Lots of people were eye witnesses that Jesus was resurrected (not simply revived) three days after His crucifixion and death and stayed on this earth in a resurrection body for forty days and then ascended to heaven unto God.

The Bible recounts Jesus's resurrection and ascension (Acts 1:9; 1 Cor. 15:3-7, 20). At the end of the last days, He will come down again gloriously in clouds with His resurrection body in what is called the Second Coming (2 Thess. 4:15-17; Matt. 24:27, 30).

The above-mentioned elements of the gospel—incarnation, sacrificial salvation, resurrection and ascension, and second coming—are called the four-fold gospel. There are also the five fundamentals of the faith—inerrancy of the scriptural writings, the incarnation, sacrificial salvation, the resurrection of Jesus' body, and his second coming. When we say we believe in Jesus, the four-fold gospel and the five fundamentals describe what we believe and what we spread and propagate.

Another doctrine we must believe is commonly called the Five Points of Calvinism, also called TULIP: (1) total inability (depravity), (2) unconditional election, (3) limited atonement, (4) irresistible grace, and (5) perseverance of the saints. The theory of limited atonement or the soteriology of Calvinism asserts that only those who believe in Jesus and repent of their sins (Mark 1:15) can be forgiven through the blood of Jesus Christ. The Christian soteriology is derived from verses in the Bible such as Acts 10:43, 13:38-39, Ephesians 1:7 and Colossians

1:13-14, all of which teach that we must believe in Jesus Christ to be forgiven His blood, without having any merits. The Bible says, "To him give all the prophets witness, that through his name whosoever believeth in him shall receive remission of sins" (Acts 10:43), and "Neither is there salvation in any other: for there is none other name under heaven given among men, whereby we must be saved" (Acts 4:12). Also it is said, "If thou shalt confess with thy mouth the Lord Jesus, and shalt believe in thine heart that God hath raised him from the dead, thou shalt be saved" (Rom. 10:9). As a result, our salvation is worked out through the redemption accomplished on the cross by Jesus Christ and through our belief in Jesus: these two are a key to our salvation.

Much like a train that does not run on one track but on two, our salvation is obtained through these two: the redemption accomplished on the cross by Jesus Christ and our belief in Jesus. Therefore, our sins can never be forgiven by any human efforts or works except by Jesus, and no one can go to heaven without believing in Jesus. Titus 3:5, which is often called the essence of the salvation theory, says, "Not by works of righteousness which we have done, but according to his mercy he saved us, by the washing of regeneration, and renewing of the Holy Ghost."

Many other verses in the Bible contend that believing in Jesus is the essential precondition for being forgiven of sins and obtaining salvation. To the question "What must I do to be saved?" (Acts 16:30), the answer is "Believe on the Lord Jesus Christ, and thou shalt be saved, and thy house" (Acts 16:31; also see Hab. 2:4; Rom. 1:7). Believing in Jesus is the only way to be forgiven of sins and acquire salvation. Here, it need be briefly mentioned about salvation gotten through re-birth. according to the Bible (John 3:5).

Christian theology describes four golden chains of salvation:
(1) Election and calling (Eph. 1:4-5; 2 Tim. 1:9).
(2) Justification (Rom. 3:24, 28; Tit. 3:7).
(3) Sanctification (Acts 26:18; Eph. 5:26; 2 Cor. 4:7).
(4) Glorification (Isa. 60:7, 13; Rom. 8:30).

These are the steps by which, in terms of time, soteriology comprises three steps: past salvation, present salvation, and future salvation. God consistently saves the flesh, soul and spirit of men in the past, present and future.

Three Temporal Steps of Salvation

1. Past salvation (justification)

"For by grace are ye saved through faith; and that not of yourselves: it is the gift of God: Not of works, lest any man should boast" (Eph. 2:8-9). Two points should be noted here: that our spiritual salvation has been completely accomplished and that the salvation has not been attained through our righteous good deeds or works but through faith and the grace of God the Father (Tit. 3:5). The past salvation enables us to recover God's image, which was lost when Adam ate the fruit of the tree of knowledge. In other words, when we believe in Jesus Christ, our filthy sins are remitted through His blood so that right relationship between us and God may be restored. It is commonly called justification or salvation by faith, which is a fundamental principle of the Christian salvation theory. Salvation by faith is totally different from salvation by works. It refers to what was completely accomplished in the past. Sometimes this completed salvation means the first and last moments of salvation. An example is the robber described in Luke 23:40-43, who repented of his sins and believed in Jesus and is saved. The Bible clearly says, "The righteousness of the righteous shall not deliver him in the day of his transgression: as for the wickedness of the wicked, he shall not fall thereby in the day that he turneth from his wickedness; neither shall the righteous be able to live for his righteousness in the day that he sinneth" (Ezek. 33:12).

2. Present salvation (sanctification)
"My beloved, as ye have always obeyed, not as in my presence only, but now much more in my absence, work out your own salvation with fear and trembling" (Phil. 2:12). This verse refers to the salvation that is being working out (1 Tim. 6:12) and a life in which the Holy Spirit and Jesus Christ are living in our spirit after we are removed from spiritual death to spiritual life through our faith and were born again of water and of the Spirit (John 3:5). "Verily, verily, I say unto you, he that believeth on me hath everlasting life. I am that bread of life" (John 6:47-48). He that believes on Jesus has everlasting life means that he who does not believe does not have everlasting life. He who believes (πίστεύων in Greek; present participle in the progressive form) points to those who are continually believing. And *have* (the present tense of ἔχει) means the state of having, which implies that the everlasting life (a life in which salvation is being worked out) is continuing from the time of believing in Jesus. Only the fleshy life (ψυχή) was retained before believing in Jesus; but after believing, a resurrected life (reborn life) is gained. Having such a resurrected life implies that we also have such a faith as had by Apostle Paul (Gal. 2:20), who led a life with faith in Christ Jesus (2 Tim. 3:15; Rom. 3:21) and that we are also fighting the good fight of faith (Matt. 21:43). This process is called sanctification for spiritual maturation or sanctification of the soul. This salvation, as a process of sanctification, is not achieved

at a time but being accomplished in a gradual manner as trees or grasses are growing.

In John 13:10, Jesus said to his disciples, whose feet He was washing, "He that is washed needeth not save to wash his feet, but is clean every whit: and ye are clean, but not all." He who took a bath (has past salvation) need not wash his whole body again but washes his feet everyday (need to have present salvation; to be sanctified). The process of present salvation will continue till we resemble Jesus Christ, attain Christian perfection and our flesh dies (see 1 Cor. 15:31, Heb. 6:1-8). What is to be remembered here is that present salvation, or salvation in the process of being sanctified, implies that we have already been saved through faith but are still living in the flesh. It does not imply that spiritual salvation or justification is already attained when our sins are forgiven, but that Christians in the flesh are being sanctified day by day through their active faith.

Everlasting life is distinguished from living the life of immortality; present salvation is living the life of immortality. In this life, the greatest two commandments of love God and love your neighbor are accomplished. Following Jesus means that Christians as disciples follow the footsteps of their teacher. They as disciples not only believe in Jesus but also imitate Jesus as their role model. They do not have disguised dead faith but saving and living faith.

3. Future salvation (glorification)

"And the Lord shall deliver me from every evil work, and will preserve me unto his heavenly kingdom: to whom be glory for ever and ever. Amen" (2 Tim. 4:18).

In the last days, all human beings will be judged before God's white throne. At this time, unbelieving unforgiven sinners shall be thrown into the everlasting fire of perdition or hell and believing forgiven sinners shall be changed into a resurrection body and enter heaven and be saved (Rev. 7:10, 20:12-15). Therefore, this salvation will take place in the future. Future salvation will not be accomplished in the past or at the present but in the future after the judgment before God's white throne. Likewise, the Bible says salvation is given at intervals of time. The Bible clearly speaks that the salvation is centered on Jesus Christ, who shed His precious blood so that only Christians may enter the Kingdom of God. The Lord says, "I am the way, the truth, and the life: no man cometh unto the Father, but by me" (John 14:6).

I have shown why Christianity is the only religion to offer salvation, why only Jesus is the Savior, and why all people must believe in Jesus to be saved. Elsewhere in this book, I want to touch on (1) the ultimate purpose of believing in Jesus, (2) the goal of Christian life, and (3) what kind of life is necessary to attain the goal.

I also want to touch on the following:
- The world after death: paradise, Hades, heaven, hell (fire = the lake of fire, sulfuric fire = the lake of burning sulfur), and judgment before the white throne (Rev. 20:11)
- Resurrection, resurrection body and transformed body
- Trichotomy and dichotomy
- Some points of eschatology
- Some points of creationism and evolutionism
- Some points of theism and christology from systematic theology
- Purpose of birth and being born again

CHAPTER 2

The Goal of a Christian Life

In the preceding chapter, we discussed the ultimate purpose of believing in Jesus, a purpose that is not momentary but everlasting. In this chapter, I will touch on the goal of the life of believing Christians. This goal is not everlasting but temporary and applicable during the life in this world.

If we believe in Jesus and then instantly die, like the bandit who was crucified along with Jesus but repented and received Christ (according to the apocryphal Acts of Pilate, the criminal hanged on the right side of Jesus who repented is Dismas while the one on the left who slandered Jesus is Gestas), we will surely directly go to the paradise (Luke 23:43), but mostly believers will remain in this world for a while. Therefore, it is necessary to know how and for what shall we live the remaining life.

A Christian life is lived for God's glory: "Whether therefore ye eat, or drink, or whatsoever ye do, do all to the glory of God" (1 Cor. 10:31). The Shorter Catechism composed of 107 questions and answers prepared in the Westminster Assembly (1648), which is a believers' written confession, asks the first question, "What is the first and foremost purpose of men?" The answer is "to glorify God and permanently please God."

The Bible says that making us God's children is "to the praise of the glory of his grace, wherein he hath made us accepted in the beloved" (Eph. 1:6). And it is also said, "This people have I formed for myself; they shall shew forth my praise" (Isa. 43:21). It teaches us that the goal of our life should be to glorify God, and we should seek God's glory only no matter what we are doing (*sola deo gloria* in Latin, meaning "only God's glory").

What then are practical principles with which to seek God's glory only? Only for the sake of God's glory, we should make money, study, repair our house, eat meals, or sleep. As an occasion requires, all things must be controlled by the goal of the glorification of God. Romans 14:8-9 says, "Whether we live, we live unto the Lord; and whether we die, we die unto the Lord: whether we live therefore, or die, we are the Lord's" Here, the Lord (κύριος in Greek) refers to אדון in Hebrew, which means God the Father Jehovah.

What does God's glory mean here? It means giving top priority or focusing on something like a convex lens converges sunlight. God's glory, in other words, means *hallowing*, like in the phrase "hallowed (ἁγισθήτω in Greek; שדק in Hebrew, different from הני or shekinah) be thy name" (Matt. 6:9-13; Luke 11:2-4). Sanctifying (Num. 20:12) means separating something and dedicating it to God only so as to glorify God. And the word *glory* (δόξα in Greek) in "For thine is the kingdom, and the power, and the glory" is a noun derived from a Greek δοκεω, which means "know, believe, think," etc. So glory means walking in a belief that understands and knows God and is fit for the name of God.

The Meribah incident in the wilderness of Zin after Israel left Egypt (Numbers 20) is an example of Moses and Aaron *not* sanctifying or glorifying God: "And the Lord spake unto Moses and Aaron, Because ye believed me not, to sanctify me in the eyes of the children of Israel, therefore ye shall not bring this congregation into the land which I have given them" (Num. 20:12). They refused to obey God's commandments (Num. 27:14) and walked without the trust that is appropriate to the name of God (Num. 20:12). Moses should not have smitten the rock two times but just pointed to the rock (Num. 20:8) so that God might make water come out of it and be glorified. His focus was not on God but on making the water come out.

Moreover, Jesus taught us the meaning of God's glory in the Sermon on the Mount, saying, "Seek ye first the kingdom of God, and his righteousness; and all these things shall be added unto you" (Matt. 6:33). Here, the word *seek* is ζητειτε in Greek, which means continually seeking out what is above. The word *first* means "before everything else."

The Kingdom of God and the Kingdom of Heaven

In one Bible manuscript, "the kingdom of God and his righteousness" is changed to "the righteousness of God and his kingdom." In the Bible, *heaven* can have two meanings: the kingdom of heaven and the kingdom of God. The two are slightly different in meaning.

The kingdom of God refers to a territory where only God and his law rules and where there are no unrighteousness, sin, or works of Satan. When such a territory is established in the mind or family of the believer, that place is none other than the kingdom of God (Luke 17:20-21). It is not a visible thing, as Jesus said. God rules and takes care of not only this world but the whole creation. But this world is not the kingdom of God because it is filled with evil, unrighteousness, sin, and the works of Satan.

The kingdom of heaven is the place into which we will go after we die and are resurrected and judged (Heb. 9:27) before

God's white throne (Rev. 20:11-15). It *is* a visible place, where God rules and there is no unrighteousness, sin, or evil. And when judgment is made before God's white throne, the present universe and earth, or the first heaven and the first earth, will pass away. Revelation 21 describes heaven like this: it is foursquare and "pure gold like unto clear glass." The length of the city is as large as the breadth: twelve thousand furlongs (about 2,218 kilometers or 1,386 miles). The flat area of heaven, therefore, is about 4,666,600 square kilometers, which about 21 times as wide as the two Koreas and half the area of United States (about 9,529,063 square kilometers). The wall of the city is 144 cubits (approximately 65.6 meters or 215 feet) high. The foundation of the city is composed of twelve jewels, including jasper.

The twelve gates of the city are made of pearls. Streets inside the city are of pure gold. There is no sun or moon nor night but it always day because the glory of God (1 John 1:5) lights it (John 1:9, 8:12). Twelve angels keep the gates.

The Righteousness of God

The righteousness (δικαιοσύνη in Greek and צדקה תונק in Hebrew) of God refers to meeting Gods' standards—conformity with God. The property of God is love (1 John 4:8,16); so God's righteousness is love (αγάπη in Greek). It is His will, which He desires and demands us to do. It is none other than keeping the two great commandments: love God with all your heart and love neighbor as yourself (Matt. 22:37-38; Mark 12:30-31; Luke 10:27). Since God is not corporal but spiritual, we should love Him by loving our neighbors. For example, providing a bowl of cold water to a neighbor in a hot summer day is serving God in love. So loving neighbors is loving God and practicing God's righteousness. God's righteousness glorifies God, therefore it should be the goal of our life to seek first and attach the top priority to God's righteousness. In this way, we can glorify, as the Shorter Catechism intends. "For do I now persuade men, or God? or do I seek to please men? for if I yet pleased men, I should not be the servant of Christ" (Gal. 1:10). "Give unto the LORD, ye kindred of the people, give unto the LORD glory and strength. Give unto the LORD the glory due unto his name: bring an offering, and come before him: worship the LORD in the beauty of holiness" (1 Chr. 16:28-29).

To pursue God's righteousness, we should ask and what God's will is. As Jesus said, "My meat is to do the will of him that sent me, and to finish his work" (John 4:34). We must daily glorify God and live for His glory.

How to Glorify God

If our goal is to glorify God, how shall we lead a life for such glory? In other words, how can we give glory to God? Sometimes, Christians clap their hands in a church while they shout, "Let's give glory to God." But how much glory do they give to God in doing so? Of course, the Bible says to clap our hands and shout to God with the voice of triumph (Ps. 47:1). So, clapping hands to God cannot be wrong. Still, how much glory is the clapping to God?

Jesus taught us how to glorify God when He said, "Let your light so shine before men, that they may see your good works, and glorify your Father which is in heaven" (Matt. 5:16). He also said, "Ye are the light of the world. A city that is set on an hill cannot be hid. Neither do men light a candle, and put it under a bushel, but on a candlestick; and it giveth light unto all that are in the house" (Matt. 5:14-15). So having the light, we are obliged to shed light by spreading the gospel to the world and those who do not have light (1 Pet. 2:12). This light or belief is explained in Romans 3:22 as "even the righteousness of God which is by faith of Jesus Christ unto all and upon all them that believe: for there is no difference."

Those who believe in Jesus Christ have the righteousness of God, no matter who they are. This belief is for living for the sake of God's righteousness (Matt. 6:33). It is not self-centered but God-centered. It is not belief in human emotions and feelings but in the word of God. The fruit of this belief is the thanksgiving and joy given by the Holy Spirit and turned into the righteousness of God.

The Works of God
The Bible talks about how God's works should be done. Someone asked Jesus, "What shall we do, that we might work the works of God?" (John 6:28). Today they might have asked if they should God's works (plural) are things like cleaning the church, teaching in Sunday school, singing in choir member, spreading the gospel, and a lot more. To the question, Jesus answered that God's work (singular, not plural) is believing in him whom God has sent.

That may seem to be an extraordinary answer. But this saying of Jesus means that everything done with faith in Jesus Christ is God's work, and anything done without faith cannot be God's work. For example, say a pastor encourages members of his congregation to bring an unbeliever to church next Sunday and a deacon invites her neighbor to come and have lunch after the service. The unbeliever attends the church service and then they have lunch together. Or say a pastor asks a painter to paint the church for one hundred dollars. At the end of the day, the painter asks, "Is there any work for tomorrow?" The pastor responds, "If you distribute gospel leaflets on the street tomorrow, I will pay you another one hundred dollars." And he agrees.

In both of these cases, is it really God's work to attend church simply for having lunch or paint the church and spread the gospel for wages? It is not God's work because the work is not done due to faith in Jesus. Wages are the incentive for the painting, whether it is for a family house or a church building, and for distributing leaflets, no matter what it is for a restaurant or for a church. It is not God's work. Furthermore, when worshiping is not done because of faith in God but for the purpose of getting lunch, it is not God's work either. In contrast, it is God's work to clean a house, wash dishes, watch TV, go to sleep, and many other thing with faith in Jesus, no matter how small the faith is.

Living with faith in Jesus means walking with the awareness of being in the presence of God (in Latin, *coram deo*). The Bible says, "whatsoever is not of faith is sin" (Rom. 14:23). And "without faith it is impossible to please him" (Heb. 11:6). Even if I have a little of Jesus Christ's faith (that is, light), anything I do according to the measure of that faith is a good deed (or the righteousness of God). Doing something according to the faith means that it is in fact accomplished by Jesus Christ.

Jesus said, "whatsoever ye shall ask in my name, that will I do" (John 14:13). This means that anything can be done with the power of Jesus.

Benediction

At the end of a church service, there is usually a benediction, or blessing. Where did this originate and how should the benediction be given? To answer these questions, we must turn to Numbers 6:22-27. God orders the priests to give a particular benediction without fail during each service: "And the LORD spake unto Moses, saying, Speak unto Aaron and unto his sons, saying, On this wise ye shall bless the children of Israel, saying unto them, The LORD bless thee, and keep thee: The LORD make his face shine upon thee, and be gracious unto thee: The LORD lift up his countenance upon thee, and give thee peace. And they shall put my name upon the children of Israel, and I will bless them."

In the New Testament, a model benediction is given by the Apostle Paul in 2 Corinthians 13:14: "The grace of the Lord Jesus Christ, and the love of God, and the communion of the Holy Ghost, be with you all. Amen."

According to Numbers 6:23, the benediction should not be prayed but proclaimed (κηρύσμα in Greek) or declared. A prayer is made to God, while the benediction is blessed from God. Therefore, the benediction should not be prayed by believers to God but said or proclaimed without fail by ministers to church members in the name of Jehovah or Jesus. This is implied by the Hebrew word 'ישמו שׁבי' (meaning, 'putting my name or in my name') in Numbers 6:27.

In the New Testament age, the benediction is declared in the name of Jesus Christ (John 14:13-14), not in Jehovah's name, as in the Old Testament age. The benediction can be proclaimed only by God's selected servants or priests (in modern times, pastors), not by everyone (common saints), unlike in the cases of prayers (1 Pet. 2:9). Since the benediction is not a prayer but a declaration, it should be proclaimed by priests or pastors in the name of the Lord or Jesus Christ. (1 Kings 6:23, 27) so that Jehovah may bless believers with His mighty power. The benediction that is not declared in the name of Jesus Christ is just like a prayer offered without mentioning the only mediator between believers and God. Our prayers will be heard with the power of our mediator Jesus Christ only when they are offered in His name (John 14:13-14).

Here is a model benediction declared in the name of Jesus Christ: "Now, the grace of our Lord Jesus Christ, who is our way, truth and life; and the everlasting love of Jehovah God the Father who is 'alpha' and 'omega' and the source of love and blessing; and the protection, communion and fullness of the Holy Spirit be everlastingly with all of the Lord's beloved children participating in this service and their families in our Lord Jesus Christ's name. Amen."

In giving the benediction, the essentials (κλείς in Greek) are (1) declaring (that is, saying, not praying) (2) in the name of Jesus Christ (in the Old Testament, Jehovah's name) and (3) that it should be given by pastors during services. God, who is the source of blessing, blesses the congregation in response to the benediction, which must be given in Jesus Christ's name. The benediction given without mentioning Jesus Christ's name is of no avail.

True faith leads without fail to good works and obedience. Works are the results of the practical faith of a changed life. Works are not the key to salvation (Tit. 3:5) because our salvation is dependent upon the forgiveness of our sins. Rather, good works and obedience demonstrate that our faith is alive, not dead. Our works cannot bring about the forgiveness of our sins.

Conditions for Going with the Lord

There are preconditions for us to follow our Lord. First, there must be self-denial. The Bible says about the self, "For all that is in the world, the lust of the flesh, and the lust of the eyes, and the pride of life, is not of the Father, but is of the world" (1 John 2:16).

These three are closely related in human beings. They were the tests offered to Eve when she was tempted by the serpent to take the fruit of the tree of knowledge (Gen. 3:6): the tree was good for food (lust of the flesh) it was pleasant to look at (lust of the eyes) and it was said to make one wise (the pride of life).

There were also three temptations offered by the devil to Jesus, who had fasted forty days and nights in the wilderness (Matt. 4:1-11): to command that stones be made bread was the lust of the flesh; to cast Himself down from a pinnacle of the temple was the lust of the eyes; and being tempted with all the kingdoms of the world was the pride of life. Like the law of gravity, these three lusts tempt all of us all the time.

The Bible asks, "'Can the Ethiopian change his skin or the leopard his spots?" (Jer. 13:23). No, we cannot remove the three lusts. But Jesus commands us to deny our self and be filled with the Holy Spirit. Denying one's self means an absence of one's ego and being aware of only the Lord (in Latin, *coram deo*, meaning "God's presence"). We are absorbed in the Lord and concentrate all our thoughts and actions on God. We are aware that we are always before God.

Self-denial cannot be realized through our efforts. We may say we will deny ourselves and throw away our possessions, but in practice we cannot. We boast that we will empty our self and be rid of our obsessions, like Buddhism commands, but we can never do so completely, no matter what efforts we make. Our enthusiasm is not enough and our zeal is just void. As the Bible says, "Because the carnal mind is enmity against God: for it is not subject to the law of God, neither indeed can be" (Rom. 8:7). Based on our own effort, it is not possible to be subject to God's law.

Our self must be broken down, which, from the perspective of the world, is impossible. Did Jesus, then, command us to do what is impossible? Is there no way for us to do that? In such a dire state, the Apostle Paul, a pioneer of our faith, says with a sigh, "But I see another law in my members, warring against the law of my mind, and bringing me into captivity to the law of sin which is in my members" (Rom. 7:23-24). He declares the truth he has grasped on how to lead a reborn life: "I am crucified with Christ: nevertheless I live; yet not I, but Christ liveth in me: and the life which I now live in the flesh I live by the faith of the Son of God, who loved me, and gave himself for me" (Gal. 2:20). Paul confesses in faith that Christians cannot but live in the flesh while believing in Jesus, being crucified along with Jesus, and having the faith of Jesus. (In the Korean Bible, *faith* is expressed by a verb, but in the original language and in English versions, it is in a noun.)

This means that our self is crucified and our new being is living in the light of Jesus. "Here is the patience of the saints: here are they that keep the commandments of God, and the faith of Jesus" (Rev. 14:12). The key words of the theology of Apostle Paul are *in Christ*, which means a life in Jesus. Paul confesses in Philippians 1:21, "For to me to live is Christ," which implies that Paul's life itself is his union with Christ according to the will of Jesus Christ. We cannot defeat this world through our own efforts or power. "For whatsoever is born of God overcometh the world: and this is the victory that overcometh the world, even our faith" (1 John 5:4). This implies that we can only overcome the world when we have Christ in us and are born again. "We know that whosoever is born of God sinneth not; but he that is begotten of God keepeth himself, and that wicked one toucheth him not" (1 John 5:18). Philippians 4:7 says, "And the peace of God, which passeth all understanding, shall keep your hearts and minds through Christ Jesus."

Born Again

What do we mean by being born again and how does it happen? In John 3, Jesus says to Nicodemus, "Except a man be born again, he cannot see the kingdom of God" (John 3:3). He also says, "Except a man be born of water and of the Spirit, he cannot enter into the kingdom of God" (John 3:5). Here *the Spirit* is πνεύματος in Greek, the word used in John 4:24. This is not the Holy Spirit but the Spirit of God, which, in the Bible, it is expressed in eight ways: (1) the Spirit of God (Gen. 1:2; Isa. 61:1; Rom. 8:9), (2) the Spirit of Christ (Rom. 8:9; Phil. 1:19), (3) the Spirit of Jesus (Acts 16:7; Phil. 1:19), (4) the Spirit of His son (Gal. 4:6), (5) the Holy Spirit or the Holy Ghost (Acts 1:2, 8), (6) my spirit, meaning the spirit of a human being (Luke 23:46; Acts 7:59), (7) the Spirit of the Lord (2 Isa. 61:1; Cor. 3:17-18), and (8) the Spirit representing God the Father (John 4:24). In summary, the Holy Spirit is derived from the word 'άγιο πνεύμα' or 'άγιυ πνεύμα' in Greek.

In the Korean Bible, it is mentioned not as 'the Holy Spirit' but as the Spirit (John 3:5; Gal. 5:22). Therefore, being born of water and of the Spirit means being born again of not the Holy Spirit but God's Spirit (Joel 2:28-29; Isa. 61:1; Acts 2:17; Rom. 8:9,11; 2 Cor. 5:5). In the Old Testament, there is no such term as *Holy Spirit*. Also it is said that God the Father, translated as the Holy Spirit or the Spirit in the Korean Bible, has sent the Spirit of the Son of God (Jesus Christ's Spirit) into our hearts (Gal. 4:6). And in Acts 5:32, it is said that God gave the Holy Ghost to those who obey God the Father.

The term *being born again* (John 3:3) is derived from the Greek words γεννηθη ανωθεν: γεννηθη, meaning "being born" and ανωθεν, meaning "from above" or "again." So being born again means being born from above or being born of God anew and again, as a spiritual regeneration or new birth. This saying is not uttered without meaning or intention. No word of Jesus is unimportant, and anything He says is God's inerrant word (according to the theory of the Inerrancy of Scriptural Writings). No one can enter the kingdom of heaven unless he is born again, unless we come to believe in Jesus and then immediately die, like a the criminal who was crucified with Jesus and repented.

But Jesus also said, "Except a man be born of water and of the Spirit (not the Holy Spirit), he cannot enter into the kingdom of God"? (John 3:5). What is meant by *water* in this verse?

The water (or seed) refers to the word λόγος in Greek, as is used in "Being born again, not of corruptible seed, but of incorruptible, by the word of God, which liveth and abideth for ever" (1 Pet. 1:23). In Mark 4:14 and Luke 8:11, "the seed is the word of God." This word is none other than Jesus Christ (John 1:14). So Jesus says, "the words that I speak unto you, they are spirit, and they are life" (John 6:63). Then, who is the water?

According to 1 John 5:6, the water refers to Jesus Christ. "This is he that came by water and blood even Jesus Christ." In the Greek, "water and blood is Jesus Christ." That Jesus is spiritual water is attested in many places in the Bible, including John 4:10-14 and 7:37-38, and Revelation 21:6.

First Peter 3:21 implies that the water we are baptized in is not normal water (H_2O) but spiritual water that is Jesus: "The like figure whereunto even baptism doth also now save us (not the putting away of the filth of the flesh, but the answer of a good conscience toward God,) by the resurrection of Jesus Christ." Paul writes: "In whom also ye are circumcised with the circumcision made without hands, in putting off the body of the sins of the flesh by the circumcision of Christ: Buried with him in baptism, wherein also ye are risen with him through the faith of the operation of God, who hath raised him from the dead" (Col. 2:11-12). Those who are baptized along with Christ are clothed in Jesus Christ (Gal. 3:2). "For as yet he was fallen upon none of them: only they were baptized in the name of the Lord Jesus" (Acts 8:16) teaches that water baptism is not receiving the Holy Spirit and being born again.

Water symbolizes life; no living thing can exist without water. Jesus says that no one can enter the kingdom of God unless he or she is born again of the spiritual water, which is Jesus Christ and the Holy Spirit. Jesus and Paul clearly tell us what is "being born again."

In John 15, the Lord teaches about a grapevine (grape meant everlasting life in ancient times). He implies that the grapevine is Himself, the branches are His followers, and the husbandman is God the Father. If a branch is loosely attached to the grapevine or separated from it, the branch cannot bear fruit and eventually will be cast into the fire and burned. The branches must be connected to the grapevine, which supplies nutrition so that the branches may bring forth leaves and bear fruit. The grapevine, meanwhile, is taken care of and its branches pruned by the husbandman, who is God the Father.

Being born again can be illustrated by the following example. When the farmer plants a seed from a large and sweet persimmon, the fruit the seed brings forth is not a large and sweet persimmon but a small and bitter one (wild persimmon). The farmer says, "It is very strange. Clearly I planted a large and sweet persimmon, but the fruit is not." He plants a second time, but the result is the same. This applies to a pear and an olive tree as well. In order to make the tree bring forth a good fruit, it must be grafted.

So we are told by Paul in Romans 11:17: "And if some of the branches be broken off, and thou, being a wild olive tree, wert graffed in among them, and with them partakest of the root and fatness of the olive tree." In other words, if a dead tree is grafted into a tree of life, then it will be given a new life.

The Heidelberg Catechism, published in February 1563, says about rebirth that "It is being grafted into the Holy Spirit or Christ." And the Shorter Catechism of Westminster and the Westminster Confession of Faith teaches that rebirth is "to apply to us the redemption paid and bought by Christ through the Holy Spirit who uses His effective call to rouse up faith within us and join us unto Christ." Being born again is the combination and union of the Holy Spirit or Christ's Spirit with our spirit. "And because ye are sons, God hath sent forth the Spirit of his Son into your hearts, crying, Abba, Father" (Gal. 4:6). Therefore, being born again means being born of God's Spirit and God's word. If we are born again, the seed (1 Pet. 1:23) of the Bible or word is planted and gradually grows within us. Our real nature cannot be changed by our power but only by the Holy Spirit or Jesus Christ's Spirit. When the Spirit abides in me and I am grafted into the Spirit, then my evil old nature is banished and changed into a new good one. We can be changed only by the power of the Holy Spirit and Christ. Jesus says, "I am the vine, ye are the branches: He that abideth in me, and I in him, the same bringeth forth much fruit: for without me ye can do nothing" (John 15:5). This grafting occurs when we are crucified along with Jesus and resurrected along with Him.

Being born again is different from being reformed or remodeled. It is a change in our nature. The Holy Spirit dwells in us and we are newly grafted into Christ. Paul calls such a changed person "a new being" (2 Cor. 5:17). First Peter 1:23 says, "Being born again, not of corruptible seed, but of incorruptible, by the word of God, which liveth and abideth for ever."

As an egg gives birth to a life when it is fertilized, so we will be born again when the word, the seed of life, is planted in us.

Paul further tells us, "But ye are not in the flesh, but in the Spirit, if so be that the Spirit of God dwell in you. Now if any man have not the Spirit of Christ, he is none of his" (Rom. 8:9). The Spirit of Christ is the word of Christ, as is implied in John 6:63: "The words that I speak unto you, they are spirit, and they are life." Paul writes, "And because ye are sons, God hath sent forth the Spirit of his Son into your hearts, crying, Abba, Father" (Gal. 4:6).

The Apostle John writes, "And this is the record, that God hath given to us eternal life, and this life is in his Son. He that hath the Son hath life; and he that hath not the Son of God hath not life" (1 John 5:11-12). "He that hath the Son" means he that hath Jesus Christ's Spirit (Rom. 8:9), which is the word (John 6:63), and the words of Bible verses planted in our mind.

In Galatians 5, the Apostle Paul talks not about the Holy Spirit but spirit of Jesus Christ, which is Christ's word. The nine fruits of Christ's Spirit are love, joy, peace, longsuffering, gentleness, goodness, faith, meekness, and temperance. Paul implies that we must be born again of Christ's Spirit, His word. What is to be remembered is that the husbandman doing the grafting is God the Father. Therefore, being born again does not occur by our power. It is God's grace and gift. "So then it is not of him that willeth, nor of him that runneth, but of God that sheweth mercy" (Rom. 9:16). We are born again and changed only when God the Father puts the Holy Spirit or Christ's Spirit into us (2 Cor. 5:5, 1:21-22; Phil. 2:13; 1 Pet. 1:3).

Rebirth, then, is not building character through moral training, nor is it enlightenment achieved by human efforts like meditation or awakening. Rather it is accomplished when God's seed is planted in us and we are newly born and changed.

As Jesus told his apostles, "But ye shall receive power, after that the Holy Ghost is come upon you" (Acts 1:8). Being born again is done by the power and authority of the Holy Spirit. As darkness automatically gives way when light shines, so evil gives in when the Holy Spirit is come.

In Mark 10:25-27, Jesus says that it is easier for a camel to go through the eye of a needle than for a rich man to enter into the kingdom of God. "And they were astonished out of measure, saying among themselves, Who then can be saved? And Jesus looking upon them saith, With men it is impossible, but not with God: for with God all things are possible." With purely human efforts, we cannot keep our resolutions longer than a few days.

But, all things are possible with those who are born again. As Paul says, "Therefore if any man be in Christ, he is a new creature: old things are passed away; behold, all things are become new" (2 Cor. 5:17). Those born again are changed and lead a new life. If we are born again, our nature is changed and our life is transformed. If we are born again, we can lead a sinless life. It is not possible through our own efforts of moral discipline or training but only because God's seed is planted and is growing in us. "Whosoever is born of God doth not commit sin: for his seed remaineth in him; and he cannot sin, because he is born of God" (1 John 3:9). Paul says in Romans 8:1-2: "There is therefore now no condemnation to them which are in Christ Jesus, who walk not after the flesh, but after the Spirit. For the law of the Spirit of life in Christ Jesus hath made me free from the law of sin and death." It means that those born again of the Holy Spirit and Jesus Christ will not commit a sin. A persimmon tree cannot be changed as soon as it is grafted, but the seed grows gradually until it bears large and sweet fruit. In the same manner, after being born again, we lead a changed life through a sanctification process while the seed of Christ's word is growing in us.

As Jesus says in the parable of the man scattering seeds (Mark 4:26-28), we do not know how the seed grows. "But the earth bringeth forth fruit of herself; first the blade, then the ear, after that the full corn in the ear." This shows why we say that justification is a momentary process, but sanctification is continuing. When we are born again and led by the Holy Spirit each day, we will be changed new everyday since God's seed is growing in us. Our life will be ceaselessly renewed, changed newer and continuously growing in faith till we die. Paul says in 1 Corinthians 15:31, "I die daily." And he also confesses, "For which cause we faint not; but though our outward man perish, yet the inward man is renewed day by day." He also says, "Not as though I had already attained, either were already perfect: but I follow after, if that I may apprehend that for which also I am apprehended of Christ Jesus" (Phil. 3:12). This verse describes the process of his sanctification.

The faith of those born again differs in shape and volume among believers. One may be "round," another "square" and still another "triangular" in shape. One may be 60 and another 90 or 120 in volume. So, it is stated in the Bible, "to think soberly, according as God hath dealt to every man the measure of faith" (Rom. 12:3) and "according to the proportion of faith" (Rom. 12:6). This kind of faith is not related to our salvation but to our works being done for God.

It is a practical matter that when we are born again and become a new being (2 Cor. 5:17), following the footsteps of Jesus who had such faith, we are given a gift of God (Eph. 2:8) and lead a changed life everyday according to the proportion of faith. Our mind-set affects our thinking; our behavior is dependent on the positive or negative attitude of our thinking;

our behavior leads to our habits, which result in our character and decides our destiny. Therefore, everything is dependent upon our mind-set, which is given by God, as the Holy Spirit works on us. We can receive the Holy Spirit when we obey God (Acts 5:32) and His word revealed in the Bible. We must say yes when the Bible says yes and no when the Bible says no.

God puts the Holy Spirit and Jesus Christ into us so that we may be born again (Rom 5:5, Gal. 4:6). And the Holy Spirit and Jesus Christ dwells in our heart "that Christ may dwell in your hearts by faith" (Eph. 3:17). The heart is called the center of our conscience. When we feel guilty, first of all, our heart will pound and beat. Therefore, when we are born again, we will get rid of our sin-senseless conscience seared with a hot iron and have a new heart. Being born again of Jesus Christ is crucifying myself and cutting off the cord that connects me with the world. Then, our values and preferences are changed so that we give up what we have relied on and listen to God's voice first and follow His word. Just as Abraham left his home in Haran in compliance with God's word and was blessed (Gen. 12:1-7), so if I am born again, I should also leave my old life and lead a new one.

One way to objectively determine if a person is born again is to note if he or she can give thanks. Those who do not give thanks have not been born again and do not have faith, which is shown in obeying the word of God. Obedience is different from submission. Submission is a conforming action even though the mind is not willing, while obedience is an action done in a willing mind. Therefore, those who are born again do not submit themselves but rather obey the word of God. Without fail, being born again must be implemented by the Holy Spirit and Christ's Spirit.

In the twenty-first century, a most conspicuous problem in society seems to be a numbness to immorality. In this age, there are many church members, who desire to lead not a life of faith as a Christian but a religious life in order to be successful in this world. Why is it that there are so many churches in the world and yet social morals are broken down? It is because there are many believers who believe in only in their heads but are not born again of the Holy Spirit and the light of Jesus. "Thou hast a name that thou livest, and art dead" (Rev. 3:1). Those who are alive are different from those dead in that the former is willing to give thanks while the latter is not.

If we are born again, we must take up our cross daily and follow Jesus (Luke 9:23). In this world, each person lives in different circumstances. Some are suffering from physical or mental illnesses. Some are agonizing under financial difficulties or starvation. Some are groaning because of family problems or troubles in their workplace. Each of us lives in the conditions as God has dealt to us according to the measure of faith. our Anyone who is wise does not blame others but tries to be content with what he or she has, no matter how heavy a cross he or she bears. Anyone who is wise holds the faith (light) given by God, follows the footsteps of Jesus, and goes to heaven.

The Bible commands, "Thou shalt love the Lord thy God with all thy heart, and with all thy soul, and with all thy strength, and with all thy mind; and thy neighbour as thyself" (Luke 10:27; Matt. 22:37-38). At this, a certain lawyer asks, "Who is my neighbour?" (Luke 10:29). In response, Jesus tells a story of a good Samaritan, a priest and a Levite. Then, He asks, "Which now of these three, do you think, was neighbour unto him that fell among the thieves?" (Luke 10:36). From this story, we learn who our neighbor is. My neighbors are not those who are near me but those who ask a favor of me or provide help to me irrespective of the distance between me and them. Those who need my help or give me help are my true neighbors.

The Bible teaches that neighbors have nothing to do with the distance of separation. Often we say, "There is a close relationship between him and me," or "He is far from me." Here, *close* or *far* refers not to the physical distance but to a mental affection. My neighbors, then, are not determined by physical distance. In this sense, God commands us to love our neighbors.

But how do I love my neighbors? I must treat them the same way as I love myself. What is good to me is good to others and vice versa. The same thing is recorded in the Analects of Confucius (551 - 479 BC): "Do not order others to do what I do not want to do." More positive and active than this is the Bible's "golden rule" of Jesus: "All things whatsoever ye would that men should do to you, do ye even so to them: for this is the law and the prophets" (Matt. 7:12). Counseling theories contend that loving others is pleasing others.

As the shape of the cross implies, we must vertically love God for the sake of God's glory and righteousness of God while we horizontally love our neighbors as we love ourselves.

Jesus life and ministry are summarized in His new commandment, which is also called the key to the gospel, recorded in John 13:34: "A new commandment I give unto you, That ye love one another; as I have loved you, that ye also love one another." A Christian's life is one of self-denial and is identified by serving others. We live according to the direction of the Holy Spirit, as commanded in Philippians 2:5, "Let this mind be in you, which was also in Christ Jesus." In life we also consider what Jesus would think, say, or do, making Him our role model, imitating Him (Rom. 15:5) and "looking unto Jesus" (Heb. 12:2).

The born-again life is led by the person in whom Jesus dwells (1 Pet. 1:23). Being born again is not like the moon, which reflects light, but like the sun, which sheds light. Jesus Christ's original light (John 8:12, 12:46) is totally different from the light we have received from Jesus Christ. Jesus Christ is a luminous body, like the sun or God the Father (1 John 1:5). While we are not the form of God but the moon, which reflects the light of the sun. However, even though we are the moon, we do not play a passive role but an active one, like the sun. The Bible says, "Ye are the light of the world" (Matt. 5:14); "Ye are all the children of light and the children of the day" (1 Thes. 5:5); "For ye were sometimes darkness, but now are ye light in the Lord: walk as children of light" (Eph. 5:8); and "Let your light so shine before men, that they may see your good works, and glorify your Father which is in heaven" (Matt. 5:16). We must not try only to imitate or emulate Jesus Christ but be grafted onto Him so that the Holy Spirit and Christ's word may dwell in us and the seed may be planted in us.

Conclusion

This chapter draws three conclusions: First, the ultimate reason to believe in Jesus is the salvation of our souls (1 Pet. 1:9). Second, the goal of a Christian life is to glorify God (1 Cor. 10:31) and to seek for His righteousness (Matt. 6:33). Third, living a life for God's glory requires being born again (John 15:4-5; Rom. 11:17) since such a life is impossible unless we are "a new creature" (2 Cor. 5:17).

Being born again requires that the Holy Spirit or Jesus Christ's Spirit should come into us (Rom. 8:9), which is only made possible by God the Father (John 6:44, 65, 15:1; Rom. 3:24; Eph. 2:8). We can lead the life God requires of us only when, as born again Christians, we act according to the measure of faith we have and serving others, thinking, speaking, and acting like Jesus would.

What does it mean to live in correct relationship with God? It is a life aware that no matter who else is beside us, God always stands with and watches us. Christians should live, as Jesus says (Luke 9:23), denying themselves and bearing their own cross.

I am sure that when we stand before God, the only question He will ask us is, "Have you led a life of faith in Jesus?" Our faith is determined by its fruits. "Ye shall know them by their fruits. Do men gather grapes of thorns, or figs of thistles?" (Matt. 7:16).

In Matthew 22:11-12, those permitted to attend the marriage feast are arrayed in a wedding garment. This wedding garment is the righteousness of saints (Rev. 19:8) and the robe of righteousness (Isa. 61:10). Putting on this garment means being born again or being a new creature (Gal. 6:15). We can not wear the garment unless we are born again, no matter how much effort we have made. That is why it is said that a way to hell is wide and smooth while a way to heaven is narrow and rugged (Matt. 7:13-14).

We all must seriously look at our past, set new goals for our life, and be assured that Jehovah, the Lord of hosts, walks with us. We will then journey toward heaven, which is our ultimate goal.

CHAPTER 3

The Doctrine of Man

Systematic theology is a set of biblical teachings about theological themes arranged in such a manner that students may correctly understand the holy scriptures. A modern designation of it is dogmatics. Systematic theology, which is taught in most seminaries, offers systematic explanations of many biblical revelations recognized by Christianity.

Systematic theology or dogmatics is grouped into various doctrines as stated below:

(1) Doctrine of Scripture

(2) Doctrine of God

(3) Doctrine of Christ

(4) Doctrine of the Holy Spirit

(5) Doctrine of man

(6) Doctrine of the church

(7) Doctrine of sin

(8) Doctrine of salvation, also called soteriology

(9) Doctrine of the future, also called eschatology

(10) Doctrine of angels and Satan

(11) Doctrine of heaven and hell

Before everything else, here are some important points of the doctrine of man. First, we must abide by a principle that the inerrancy of the scriptural writings should be accepted in order to understand and explain the Bible, which is the word of God. Second, any existing preconceptions should be disregarded. One must study scripture with a new mind.

Hermeneutics is the study of the principals of biblical interpretation. It comprises methods of objective and subjective interpretation, which can be undertaken from perspectives such as social, historical, and cultural. Depending upon the context in which the Bible is interpreted, there are also a compositional interpretation method and a prophetic one. There is a method to interpret scripture in terms of allusive implications and another method to shed historical light on the grammar and context. There are literal and metaphorical interpretation methods. To aid interpretation, there are numerous interpretational references and commentaries that offer expiations and glosses. Traditionally, biblical interpretation methods have stressed research into etymology, grammar, sentence structure, and context, and its historical situations.

In Wheaton, Illinois, near Chicago, the Korean World Mission Council meets every four years the Billy Graham Center on the campus of Wheaton College. A slogan used at the center is 'The Bible Says,' emphasizing that the words are not the sayings of Billy Graham but of the Bible. The sayings of the Bible is absolutely authoritative but that of Karl Barth, Emil Brunner, Rudolf Bultmann, Oscar Cullman, or Hermann Gunkel are not. In these days, people are inclined to consider the Bible as a myth and give more authority to human assertions. But Christians ought to trust the words of the Bible much more than the sayings of people. We must trust only the Bible (*sola scriptura*, in Latin), focus on only faith (*sola fide*) and operate in grace only (*sola gratia*) for the ultimate purpose of God's glory (*sola deo gloria*).

The Bible must always be interpreted in the proper context. Atheists often confront believers with a question like, "Why don't you believe that the Bible says 'There is no God'?" A believers may ask, "Where in the Bible is there such a saying?" The unbeliever replies, "If I point to a verse that asserts there is no God, will you disown the existence of God?" Then, they may point to Psalms 14:1, "The fool hath said in his heart, There is no God." While the verse does contain the sentence, "There is no God," the context makes clear that it is part of a fool's contention. However, never does the Bible confirm that there is no God.

Here is another example. Atheists tell believers not pray because the Bible says, "Therefore pray not thou for this people, neither lift up cry nor prayer for them, neither make intercession to me" (Jer. 7:16). Are the atheists correct? This Bible verse was given by God when He was angry with Israel. Is it applicable to other conditions? Is it right to claim that the Bible says there is no God because we read "Where is your God?" in Psalms 42:3? Never! It is ridiculous to read a Bible verse without attention to a whole sentence and its context. Correctly interpreting a Bible verse requires not only knowing the correct context, it also requires knowing about wrong preconceptions and explanation that nonbelievers use.

The Theory of Evolution
As long as we are caught in the fabrication that monkeys evolved into humans, we cannot understand God's word correctly. How on earth can a monkey be turned into a man, and how can a stone image be changed into a human being? Evolution is a fabricated fiction that contends that protein (a granule of protein is composed of at least twenty amino acids)

was generated from sea water. These granules of protein gathered and changed into a living thing. In 1859, Charles Robert Darwin (1809-1882) published *On the Origin of Species by Means of Natural Selection,* which asserts that something has evolved from nothing and man from monkey. Evolution is fundamentally different from change, yet the theory contends that mutations have led to changes in creatures that evolved until a higher animal appears. If a monkey is mutated into a hare and a hare into a frog, it is not evolution but degeneration. If a man is changed again into a monkey, it is not evolution but degeneration. What is important in the theory of evolution is that in principle, mutation must lead to not degeneration but evolution only.

Generally, geologists say that the earth appeared during the "big bang" 5.3 billion years ago and that creatures came into being about one billion years ago. Especially, in the Cambrian period (about 500 million years ago), many kinds of creatures appeared in large quantities. According to evolutionists, creatures appeared in a sequence that went from plants, to fish or shellfish, amphibians, reptiles, birds, and then mammals, from which came primates including human beings. Various geological strata and creatures appeared in each of the geological ages, such as the Proterozoic, the Paleozoic, the Mesozoic, and the Cenozoic. However, none of these contentions can be verified. They are like a scenario in a novel and no more than a fanciful fiction. No geological stratum or fossil is demonstrably assigned to a specific geological age because fossils are found even in a geological stratum belonging to the other eras. In other words, strata of different eras are mixed together. We are so familiar with this fabricated theory that we do not dare to question it.

In the United States, Mount Saint Helens stands next to Mt. Adams about 96 miles (80 kilometers) south of Seattle. The mountain's volcanic peak erupted on May 18, 1980. Lava swept large trees down into the Spirit Lake north of the volcano. In about three months, after the lava was cooled down, the trees were excavated and turned into coke, which is an initial form of coal. This scene scientifically disproves the existing theories that coal can be formed over millions of years. There is a radiation clock (usually, a carbon isotope clock is used), which is used to measure the age of a geological stratum or fossil. The carbon isotope clock has a great error range and is not reliable. For example, a twig may be measured to have appeared ten thousand years ago. The so-called radio-carbon dating methods using nuclear fission metals (which are decomposed into lead, argon number 40 or argon number 36 through uranium) are applicable on the assumption that deposits are composed of parent elements and parent elements, in which magma is cooled down, will change into daughter elements, whose atomic counts are lower, and will collapse while gradually losing electrons. They contend that such measuring methods are quite scientific and accurate since the said error range is meaningless.

However, there is a case that shows that samples taken out of the center of a one-thousand-year-old volcano were measured to be millions of years old because a decision has to be made about the ratio between parent elements and daughter elements. In another case, three clear footprints of a dinosaur were found on the Paluxy riverbed in the Dinosaur Valley in Glen Rose, Texas. Just above the dinosaur footprints, there were also clear footprints of men, which seems to disprove the fabricated story that dinosaurs had existed in the Jurassic period, 6.5 million years before men existed. That footprints of men are left just over those of dinosaurs shows that human beings existed along with the dinosaurs. The theory of evolution contends that human beings appeared less than about three million years ago, but how can it be explained that footprints of men appeared along with those of dinosaurs about six million years ago? The theory of evolution asserts that dinosaurs became extinct about 6.5 million years ago and human beings began to appear three million years ago.

We must not trust the false theory of evolution. Let me call your attention to a research article found in the Proceedings of the National Academy of Sciences, issued in 1997. The report describes how researchers from Montana State University observed blood cells of dinosaurs extracted from leg bones of a tyrannosaurus, which had not yet become a fossil. What does it mean that blood cells of dinosaurs extracted from non-hardened leg bones of a tyrannosaurus living 6.5 million years ago have not yet become a fossil? It implies that the dinosaur had existed during the age of Noah and the flood, about 2558 BC. Today's science has demonstrated that dinosaurs did not disappear till about five thousand years ago, after the deluge and after climate and environmental conditions changed abruptly and drastically. It is conjectured that the animal mentioned as a behemoth in Job 40:15 is in fact a dinosaur. The term *dinosaur* was not used till 1840, and a dinosaur is designated as a behemoth in the King James Version published in 1611. Moreover, many old pictures in caves or on rocks around the world have dinosaurs, not behemoths.

They say that the so-called Jurassic shrimp became extinct fifty million years ago. However, this shrimp is found in waters of the Sargasso Sea in the North Atlantic. And the bat, which is said to have appeared about 1.1 million years ago, has not evolved or changed at all. Isn't it nonsense that a monkey evolved into a man about three million years ago while a bat has remained the same for the last 1.1 million years? Furthermore, why is it that some monkeys are still living on earth if monkeys have been evolved into and substituted by men through natural selection in accordance with to the theory of evolution? Why is it that DNA of creatures in an amber, which is called an ancient pumpkin and said to have appeared about two billion years ago, has not been damaged but preserved intact? All these questions disprove the theory of evolution, which contends that all creatures have evolved into what they are today over a startlingly long period of time. On the contrary, they prove that about 1.5 million kinds of animals have appeared over a shorter period of time and that the present earth appeared during a period of no more than scores of months in diastrophism or climate changes.

Isn't it easier to try to bury your head in the sand than to believe the theory of evolution? Today, when the world has been greatly enlightened, we must rid ourselves of such a fabrication as soon as possible. Evolution asserts that cultures of human beings (*homo sapiens*) developed during the Old Stone Age, when anthropoid apes appeared, and during the New Stone Age, the Bronze Age, and the Iron Age. More concretely, the ages comprise the Oldowan Stone Age, when *homo habilis* used tools for the first time about two million years ago, the Achulian Stone Age when *homo erectus* lived, about one million years ago, the Mousterian Stone Age when Neanderthal man lived, 600,00 to 350,000 years ago, the Bronze Age, 4000-2000 BC, and the Iron Age, 1200 to 1000 BC.

That human beings did not evolve from monkeys or gorillas is demonstrated by the Lucy fossils of Australopithecus, living about 3.20 million years ago or in the early part of the diluvia epoch. Lucy is said to be a direct ancestor of the humans found in the Awash river valley, Ethiopia, a desert region where the Ardi fossils formed 4.4 million years ago and also excavated in 1992.

The fossil of a woman living about five million years ago, in the late Miocene period, is academically called *Ardipithecus Ramidus,* whose nickname is Ardi, shows that the woman about four feet (120) tall and weighed about 110 pounds (50), had short legs and long arms and walked erect. In contrast, Lucy was about three feet (90) tall. These fossils demonstrate that human beings did not evolve from monkeys but started to walk erect from the beginning like Lucy and Ardi. Denisova a primitive man discovered in Denisova in the Altai Mountains, Russia came out from Africa and concurrently lived along with Neanderthal men till about four million years ago. The Neanderthal man found in the Neanderthal cave in Dusseldorf, Germany, was considered a primitive man since his back is curved. However, a thorough examination determined that the Neanderthal man was hunchbacked because of lack of vitamin D.

Sometimes, a self-claimed archeologist skillfully assembles bones of an orangutan with those of a human being to produce the bones of a primitive man. Or, a skull and jawbones are ground and worn out by evolutionists with a metal wire so as to fabricate a anthropoid ape or primitive man. Hujimura Sinichi, a Japanese amateur archaeologist, announced a discovery later shown to be a forgery. In October 2000, he called reporters and said he had excavated something, after having buried ancient relics underground at night. But his deceptive action was revealed when it was caught by an up-to-date infrared light camera.

Modern science has exposed that almost all the anthropoid apes are false or intentionally invented. It is crystal clear that the big bang theory, which asserts that the universe was created when a lump of stone was abruptly and instantly expanded, or the theory of evolution is fabricated. It is known that the solar system has nine planets, each of which has its own satellites. For example, the earth has the moon and Jupiter has more than 135 satellites. If any of these many planets and satellites comes nearer to or farther from the sun just by a mile, the present solar system cannot exist. The system also cannot exist when there is a slight change in the size or weight of the planets and satellites or in the angle for the rotation or revolution of them.

It is a chimerical story to say that the planets and satellites of the solar system have not existed from the beginning as they are today and a stone, whose origin no one knows, rolled over and suddenly and accidentally exploded into the sun, the satellites, and the planets. The probability for the solar system to be created in such a way is startlingly lower than that for a stone image to turn into a human being and walk away in a moment. According to the Bible, God the Creator measured the distance between the planets and satellites, weighed each planet and satellite and set the size and magnitude of them (Isa. 42:5; Job 9:8-9, 26:7-14, 38:4-6; Amos 5:8; Isa. 40:22, 48:13; Psa. 104:19; Prov. 8:29; Gen. 1:14-18; Col. 1:17; Heb. 1:3). Can it be true that the size, weight, distance, angle and revolution speed of the sun, the nine planets and their satellites were naturally formed in an instant, as they are today? Modern scientists contend that the solar system was not accidentally assembled in a natural manner but was formed by a certain intellectual designer.

Now, I will briefly tell the Bible's explanations for the origins of the earth and its present changed aspects since the

Noah deluge. The initial earth before the Noah deluge was totally different from what it is today. According to the Bible, when the earth was initially created, it was not like what it is today because its surface was not hard or stony but soft and tender and formless, like molten iron in a furnace (the earth was without form and void, Gen. 1:2). Out of such a state, God the Creator produced the earth in six days. God completely covered the atmosphere of the earth with the water canopy in such a shape as the hard skin covers the soft interior of a watermelon (Gen. 1:6; Prov. 8:27). Erwin Munn and Joseph Dillow of the Moody Bible Institute estimate that the about forty-foot (12m) thick waters were above the firmament and covered the whole earth. Therefore, the temperature of the earth was always constant and changed little (men could live undressed, Gen. 3:7). And the temperature of the North Pole, the South Pole and the equator was unchanged and there was no rain and no rainbow (Gen. 2:5).

The rainbow first appeared only after the water canopy melted away and the atmosphere was greatly changed (Gen. 9:12-13). A rainbow is an optical and meteorological phenomenon that causes a spectrum of light to appear in the sky when the sun shines on droplets of moisture in the earth's atmosphere. Raining or snowing requires the formation of a trough of atmospheric pressure due to a difference in atmospheric pressures (in the weight of the air and winds, Job 28:25). A difference in atmospheric pressures is caused by a difference in the temperatures.

In the beginning, the temperature of the earth remained almost the same all the year round (Gen. 3:7, 10). It seems that harmful ultraviolet rays or infrared light from outside like sunlight were intercepted by the water canopy outside the atmosphere, so that the light might come through the water canopy (the ozone layer or sunshade, Ps. 19:4; Isa. 40:22) to human beings, plants, and animals in appropriate quantities. It is why, before the flood, the lifespan of men was almost one thousand years (Gen. 5). It seems that at that time, unlike today, no corner on the earth was very cold or very hot all the year round. What is required for the living of all animals and plants was supplied from the mist and fog rising from the earth and numerous nutrition buried in the earth (Gen. 1:7, 2:6). Unlike today, at that time, the soil of the earth was not very hard but always filled with moisture (Gen. 2:6). The soil was filled with the waters above the firmament and under the firmament (Gen. 1:7). It was like a greenhouse in which water was not sprayed over flowers but supplied into the bottom of flower pots so that flowers may remain fresh at all times.

In its original language, the term *watered* in Genesis 2:6 implies that a fountain came up from the ground. In those days, much moisture came up from the ground to make plants and trees thick so that big animals like a dinosaur might live and all the flesh-eating animals like a lion and a tiger might live on plants, like today's panda bear, which takes for food the hard skin of a bamboo tress (Gen. 1:30; Isa. 11:6-8, 65:25). Human beings and animals began to eat flesh in addition to vegetables after the flood when God permitted flesh-eating in Genesis 9:3. On the earth, the land was one piece and the sea was also only one (Gen. 1:9-10). Before the so-called Triassic period, there was the Pangaea (one united continent) which comprised one land and one sea. The earth was divided into five oceans and six continents when crustal movements like orogenic and epeirogenic movements were caused by the flood (Gen. 7:11; Prov. 3:20). During the deluge, the water canopy covering the earth melted and rained down for forty days (960 hours). Rain at the time of the Noah deluge was not a sprinkling but a pouring.

The water canopy was melted down, volcanoes were broken up not only on the land but also in the sea, the earth quaked and split, much water gushed up from the ground (Gen. 7:11), and crustal movements happened here and there. In the end, there came out five oceans and six continents as well as many islands and high mountains. A geologist contends that, like a puzzle game, North America, South America, and Africa could be combined into one great continent, which demonstrates that originally the earth was one lump. German geologist Alfred Wegener (1880-1930) in 1913 suggested the continental drift theory, which states that parts of the earth's crust slowly drifted atop a liquid core. The fossil record supports and gives credence to the theories of continental drift and plate tectonics (Gen. 7:11; Prov. 3:20). Sometimes, shells are found on the top of a mountain, which demonstrates that the mountain was previously under the sea. Such phenomena can be found in any corner around the world.

When the water canopy, which had covered the atmosphere of the earth, melted away, snowstorms raged to form icebergs in the polar regions, and the tropical region turned swelteringly hot as today (Gen. 8:22). As the water canopy, which had served as an ice box and prevented the outside temperature from changing, disappeared due to the Noah deluge, harmful infrared lights or ultraviolet rays came into the earth's environment from outside the atmosphere and the lifespan of human beings abruptly shortened. At most, if the fabricated theory of evolution is true, current science could not accept beyond this assumption that bacteria could evolve into an ameba. It is quite impossible for a human being to have evolved from nothing in 5 billion years ago since the earth came into being or even in 13.7 billions years since the universe came into being, and it is totally impossible for such a thing to happen in one billion years. When a sperm meets an egg cell, the cell is divided and multiplied in perfect order according to a given genetic program so that the head and body and all the limbs of a human may be formed in nine months. While on the contrary, the theory of evolution asserts that a human being should come simply from a cell division caused by mutations without any given genetic program. According to the theory of evolution, for instance, the first-ever baby came into being ages ago with its eyes attached to its feet.

Then, as it evolved, another baby with its eyes attached to its knees or belly came into being. In the startlingly long process of multiple stages of evolution, at last, a baby with its eyes attached onto its face came into being. Of course, such a hypothesis can be also applied to the nose or ears as well as hands. Numerous processes of mutations and trial and error have to go on until all of the body limbs and all the (approximately 60 trillion) cells of a man have evolved properly without any given genetic information. Is it a truly reliable story?

Here is another example. What about a monarch butterfly, which flies approximately 1,100 miles (1,800) from Chicago to the Gulf of Mexico to evade cold winter? It has never been there nor heard of the gulf, nor knows how to reach there, but it can fly there according to a given genetic program. How can evolution, which is totally dependent upon the assumption of mutations and trial and error, explain the behavior of the butterfly? This is applicable not only to the butterfly but also to a turtle and a salmon.

Here is a interesting mathematic story related to the probability of evolution. Once upon a time, the king asked his vassal who had been loyal to the king what kind of reward he wanted. The vassal answered, "Your majesty, please give me a grain of rice put in the first space on the chess board, a double portion in the second space, and a quadruple portion in the third space till the last space is filled in the same manner."

At the request, the king burst into a roar of laughter and said, "You are very naive and unselfish asking a handful of grains as a reward. I grant your request." Then, in a moment, a servant distributing the grains hurried into the presence of the king and said, "All the grains in the barn have been offered. However, not even half of the spaces on the chess board have been filled. Maybe all the rice in this country must be given to fill all the spaces." The king was furious and ordered it to be checked to be true or not. And it was found that about 9,223 trillion grains would be needed to fill just the 64 spaces on the board. The king was startled and yelled, "It cannot be believable!"

Then, just imagine. Can some creatures in this world evolve to be human beings? Excavated fossils do not and cannot prove the so-called macro evolution (evolution between species) nor the micro evolution (evolution within species).

The saline concentration of sea water is about 35 permillage (‰). Vegetables if preserved in sea water will be turned salty in a few days. However, sea fish will not turn salty for ever because salt cannot be absorbed through the skin of the fish but will be emitted out of the body of the fish and not accumulated in the body.

Can such a function of the fish be acquired in a moment or over a long period of time in the process of evolution? It may be accepted that an anchovy has evolved into a mackerel, but can it be true that the physical constitution of an ancient sea fish was so different from that of today's sea fish that the fish could not filter out salt but absorbed it and died? Wouldn't that mean that there were no fish in the sea before fish having the same constitution as today started to exist? These contradictory contentions prove that the theory of evolution is false. It is completely impossible that the world of chaos and disorder gradually evolved so that all creatures came to have the arranged structure we see today. It is a starkly false that human beings and all creatures in this world evolved by means of their mutations into their present forms. According to modern mathematics, there is no probability for the creatures to evolve favorably through mutations without genetic information given beforehand.

For example, what is the probability for a coliform bacillus to be created through evolution in this world? What is the probability for PPLO, the simplest coliform bacillus, to be accidentally created through evolution? They say that a coliform bacillus has about 625 pieces of protein. The probability for one piece of protein to be created from amino acid is $1/10^{114}$. So, the probability for one coliform bacillus to be created from 625 pieces of protein is $1/10^{71,250}$. Let me compare this figure with the following ones. They say that the number of sand grains in the Ganges is 10^{52}, the number of the incomprehensible is 10^{64}, the so-called largest number imaginable in the Orient is 10^{68}, and the so-called largest number (googol-plex) imaginable in the Occident is $10^{10^{100}}$. Now that the probability for one coliform bacillus to be created from 625 pieces of protein is $1/10^{71,250}$, the probability for one human being, which comprises about 60 trillion cells, to evolve from one coliform bacillus will be 1,000 trillion times as much as the said probability. This calculation is conducted using modern science to learn the mathematic probability of evolution. Here is another example that helps us understand the probability of evolution. The probability for one human being to evolve from one coliform bacillus is the same as the probability of locating a needle from among the grains of sand on this earth, on condition that an attempt to search for a needle should not be repeated or reused on the same spot while the attempt is made more than one hundred million times.

In this world, there are thirty million species of moving creatures and more than one hundred million species of plants and animals, including microorganisms. It is a sheer fanciful and imaginary story to say that today's various animals have evolved through mutations from inanimate objects like stones, without any given genetic information.

In the twenty-first century, science is developing day by day (Dan. 12:14) to reveal that evolution is false. Twenty-five years ago, I taught a comparative religion course at a theological seminary, teaching that Christianity has a linear development of time covering from the beginning to the last judgment before God's white throne, while Buddhism believes in a circular one without the starting and ending points. Some say that Christianity is a religion of the mind for love while Buddhism is of thinking for mercy. What does this mean and what is difference between the two religions? Mind is the source of knowledge, emotion, volition, and the power to distinguish between good and evil. In contrast, thinking is a source of opinion and notion that decides and discerns between thoughts. In reference to time, Buddhism speaks of perpetuity.

What is perpetuity? There is a box, whose length, width and height are the same, about ten miles (16km). The box is filled with mustard seeds and it takes a grasshopper a year to take a seed out of the box. The time span in which the box turns empty is perpetuity, which is approximately calculated 5.2 billion years. I imagine that an evolution of creatures may happen over the period of not one perpetuity but numberless times of perpetuity. I would be inclined to believe the theory of evolution if it could explain the appearance of human beings in this manner: In old days, an ameba was created when a stone rolled away and struck into another stone, making sparks. As soon as the ameba straightened its back, it turned into a frog. When the frog jumped up suddenly, it turned into a hare. When the hare hopped up suddenly, it turned into a tiger. When the tiger sprang up into the air suddenly, it turned into a man. In order for the theory of evolution to be scientifically true, it should be demonstrated through repeated observations and experiments. What does it imply that there no intermediate fossils that would prove mutations between species have been found?

Doesn't it disprove the theory of evolution, which has disguised as an angel of light and served as a servant of Satan (2 Cor. 11:14-15)? Evolutionists assert that a human body has more than 120 so-called vestigial rudimentary organs, which are degenerated and no longer necessary and which do more harm than good, like coccyx, appendix, and thyroid gland.

However, today when the most precise up-to-date machines and most modern science are developed, it is proved that men must have coccyx since, without it, men cannot sit erect and upright. Some surgeons say that appendix is not necessary at all. But modern medicine has newly discovered that appendix plays a role in protecting humans from being infected with various bacteria and planting immunity into a man while he is growing. Today when modern science is brilliantly developed, we should not tell of something just based on what we've heard but on the basis of scientific evidence.

It is regretful that the theory of evolution has brainwashed humans so that it is accepted and believed without doubts as if it were scientifically proved. Evolution is deluding the world in the same manner as shamanism and animism deceive the people. Such paganism should be avoided. Now, we must make such efforts and have such a mind-set as to clearly distinguish between light and darkness. If evolution is true, we should now see with our eyes monkeys evolving into men in any corner of the world.

While on the contrary, for more than a thousand years, we have not seen evolution or natural selection occurring. What it means is that nothing is evolving from lower animals to higher animals, not even gradually. It disapproves the theory. Why is it that men are not evolving into higher animals, not to mention monkeys evolving into men? Some evolutionists contend that evolution did happen frequently during the Jurassic Period (about 250 million to 150 million years ago) or the Cretaceous Period (about 15 million to 70 million years ago), but it ceased to happen in modern times. This is totally contradictory.

Most frequently, evolutionists cite as a proof for the theory the Galapagos Islands near to the equator in South America, where Charles Darwin observed fourteen species finches on the islands. The bird did not mutate or evolve but remains the same as it was about 160 years ago.

A horse artificially mated with a donkey gives birth to a mule, which cannot bear a young. A lioness artificially mated with a male tiger gives birth to a tigon, which cannot bear a young either, needless to say of mutation. In contrast, Mendel Gregor Johann (1822-1884) announced Mendel's law, which asserts that all creatures have genetic factors and cause genetic variation within the scope of the same species. Mendel's law has been scientifically proved.

According to one report, Darwin was spiritually impressed so much by Elizabeth Red Curtain or Lady Hope, who visited him at his house in 1881 one year before he died, that he gave up his theory and recovered his Anglican faith, which he had acquired in childhood after being baptized and for which he majored in theology at the College of Christ of Cambridge University between 1828 and 1831.

In addition, the second law of modern thermodynamics completely disapproves the theory of evolution. That is to say, the so-called theory of survival of the fittest through natural selection is in contradiction to the second law of thermodynamics, which is an expression of the natural tendency that, over time, differences in temperature, pressure, and chemical potential will equilibrate in an isolated physical system. The second law of thermodynamics, which is also called a law of energy conservation, states that the total amount of energy in an isolated system remains constant over time or is conserved over time.

According to this law, over time the quality of energy is deteriorated in such a manner that useful energy gradually becomes extinct while useless energy accumulates, like in the process of aging of men. This law says that a creatures does not evolve into a better condition but degenerates into a worse condition, which decisively disapproves the theory of evolution. Moreover, according to the same law, useful energy dwindles away over time while the total energy of the universe remains the same. It implies that the earth is filled with useless energy or becomes extinct, since it is so much old. From the state of thermodynamic equilibrium, the second law deduces the principle of the increase of entropy and explains the phenomenon of irreversibility in nature. The term *entropy* is derived from a Greek word: εν meaning "in" and τροπε meaning "turning." Therefore, entropy means "turning in," which implies that useless energy gradually becomes extinct. In other words, entropy represents the degree of disorder of the universe. According to this law, entropy over an enormously long time has increased so much that the earth should be filled with disorder. But in reality, it is not, because the earth is not that old. Evolutionism also supports the so-called dynamo theory, which proposes a mechanism by which a celestial body such as the earth or a star generates a magnetic field. Uranus, which was found by the Voyager 2 spacecraft in 1986, also has a magnetic field, which means the age of Uranus is not so long since its magnetic field should have been lost if it were enormously old.

According to evolutionism, a mutation of a species happens very seldom and, if it happens, the species does not degenerate but evolves until numerous creatures exist, like today. But common sciences can be demonstrated through experiments or observations, but historical sciences, which handle the problems of origin, can not. Evolutionists support historical sciences, which have not been and cannot be scientifically proved.

A decisively weak point of the theory of evolution is that all evolution happens accidentally and automatically. The cells, structures, and organizations of all the creatures in this world are formed accidentally, which is totally unscientific since, from the standpoint of science, any changes should be observed not only in the past but at present as well. However, evolution processes cannot be observed today. Concerning this, evolutionists make the feeble excuse that evolution is suspended in this age.

Because the theory of evolution is completely fabricated, any assertions or conjectures made by evolutionists are also false. Schools in the U.S. state of Kansas believe that evolutionism is not a fact but a hypothesis and teach the theory of evolution along with the theory of intelligent design. In other U.S. states, schools teach both the theory of evolution and the theory of creation. And in many other states, lawsuits have been against the theory of evolution. Some time ago, President George W. Bush also mentioned the theory of intelligent design.

Some scientists advocate the theory of intelligent design, which emphasizes universal intelligence is behind evolutions and claims that a creator has created all things. We should not be inclined toward evolutionism but toward creationism as well since we cannot read, interpret and study the Bible rightly and correctly when we are preoccupied with evolutionist thinking.

"In the beginning God created the heaven and the earth" (Gen. 1:1). This verse tells when, who, how and what of the creation of the universe. "The beginning" refers to a starting point of eternal space and time and suggests that God the Creator exists beyond the time and space in which we are present. God exists in καιρός, which is a Greek word meaning "divine time," in contrast to χρόνος which is human time. For example, Isaiah 42:5 records, "God the LORD created the heavens and stretched them out; he that spread forth the earth and that which cometh out of it." This verse implies that God can make time and space quick or slow, wide or narrow. This same is also implied in "one day is with the Lord as a thousand years, and a thousand years as one day" (2 Pet. 3:8).

⁜ ⁜ ⁜

The Trinity

The theological doctrine of the trinity is not tri-theism nor is it in biblical books by the apostles Paul or John. It emerged about three hundred years after the Lord ascended.

The term *trinity* (*trinitas* in Latin) was first used by Tertullianus (died ca. 230), and τριάδ in Greek, was first used by Theophilus, living in the same period as Tertullianus. This doctrine was recognized in 325 AD at the first Nicene Council. Since then, it has been the topic of debate and discussions. To put the conclusion first, the theory of trinity shall be clearly and completely determined before the white throne of God. In theology, the trinity is considered a revealed doctrine that cannot be understood by human reason. But there are various theological theories about the trinity I want to discuss. Trinity means the combination of three or the tri-unity and comprises the economic trinity, which is the manifested or revealed trinity, and the essential or immanent trinity, which asserts that one substance has three persons.

Philippians 2:6-7 says, "Who, being in the form of God, thought it not robbery to be equal with God. But made himself of no reputation, and took upon him the form of a servant, and was made in the likeness of men." The servant is the one stated in Isaiah 42:1: "Behold my servant, whom I uphold; mine elect, in whom my soul delights; I have put my spirit upon him: he shall bring forth judgment to the Gentiles" (also see Isa. 61:1). It implies that God Himself selected and upheld Jesus Christ. That is, Jesus Christ the Son of God was in the form of God before His incarnation and equal with God the Father in His divine personality. The immanent trinity means that God is one—trinity in unity, and unity in trinity. Human beings are uni-personal while God is tri-personal. As a human being has spirit, soul and body, so the trinity has God the Father, Son, and Holy Spirit. I would like to look at some other theories of the trinity.

Modalism

Friedrich Schleiemacher (1768-1834) asserted that the trinity refers to three aspects of one God: planner, revealer, and preserver. The trinity is like a three-face mirror or a three-leaf clover. It is like an actor, who may play a son on the stage, a father, or a grandfather later. A problem with this explanation is that a son cannot be played while the father or grandfather is being played. In contrast, when Jesus was baptized "He saw the Spirit of God descending like a dove" and heard a voice from heaven (Matt. 3:16,17).

Conditionalism

The divine personality is shown in a different person at a different time but it exists in the only one person. Water may be changed into rain, snow, or ice but it is still the same entity. Water can exist in different states, like a cloud, a steam, or a river. But the nature of water remains the same. And the sun, as a luminous body, gives off light and heat while it remains the same. Likewise, the trinity may be shown as the Son of God or the Holy Spirit. A tree has roots, a trunk, leaves, and branches. Likewise, God is one but has many aspects of manifestation. Only one person exists, which may be demonstrated as the Son of God at a time or the Holy Spirit at another time.

Adoptionism

When Jesus was baptized by John and rose out of the water, a voice from heaven said, "This is my beloved Son, in whom I am well pleased" (Matt. 3:17). This implies that Jesus was not the Son of God before but he was formally adopted as the Son of God at that time when he was baptized.

Monarchianism

Of the trinity, only one person can be a true monarch. God the Father is greater than the Son (John 14:28), who must submit to the Father (2 Cor. 15:28). So, God the Father is the highest.

Role Theory

In a family, the man is the husband of his wife, the father of his children, and a son to his father, just like an actor may play the son, father, or grandfather.

Subordinationism

Origen (c. 184-254) suggests that the first person is superior to the others and that the Son of God is intrinsically subordinate to God the Father (John 8:29, 9:4), and the Holy Spirit is subordinate to God the Father and God the Son. This theory was later negated by Augustine (354-430).

Modern trinitarianism largely comprises two theories: the monism, which is also called modalism, and pluralism, which is also called tri-theism, contending that there are three different persons such as God the Father, God the Son, and God the Holy Spirit.

Lastly, I will touch on *Sabellianism.* Sabellius (AD 198–217) was born in Africa and was active in Rome. This heretical thought was thriving from the third century to the fifth century. Sabellianism held that God the Father was not at all different from but equal to the Son of God. They were sure that the Virgin Mary was pregnant by God the Father, God the Father worked as a carpenter under Joseph, and it was not God's son but God the Father who was crucified to atone for the sins of human beings. It is much like dualism.

Michael Servetus (1511?-1553) living in the same period as John Calvin, was a unitarian and denied the trinity theory. He contends that supporters for the trinity are like atheists or infidels and heretics worshiping a triad of gods.

They are also sure that Jesus is separated from God the Father since after resurrection He ascended to and sat on the right of God (Matt. 22:44; Mark 16:19; Acts 7:55-56; Eph. 1:20; Col. 3:1; 1 Pet. 3:20). "And he came and took the book out of the right hand of him that sat upon the throne" (Rev. 5:7). God is not one person since Genesis 1:26 mentions "in our image, after our likeness." Therefore, God the Father cannot sit in the place of the Son of God and vice versa. God the Father, the Son of God, and the Holy Spirit are distinct from each other. God the Father is unbegotten, while God the Son is begotten, and the Holy Spirit is proceeding. God the Father is the source of all things in the universe (1 Cor. 8:6).

Still there are many other theories about the trinity. There are orthodox theological traditions of trinitarianism that contend that there is one God whose essence is one but whose person or subsistence is three that are not divided but just distinguished from each other. In other words, God the Father, the Son of God, and the Holy Spirit are one God, but God the Father is not the Son of God, nor is the Son of God the Holy Spirit. This trinity was recognized in 325 AD by the Nicene Council and the canon of the Bible was not yet determined. The canon was decided in 397 AD at the Carthage Councils.

In relation to the trinity, here is a model answer for would-be pastors taking examinations for ordination: "God is one essence but has three persons. The first person is God the Father, second the Son of God, and third God the Holy Spirit. God the Father cannot be the Son of God, nor can the Son of God be the Holy Spirit, nor can the Holy Spirit be God the Father or the only-begotten Son of God. The three persons are so established that they cannot be confused or mingled with each other. This triune God is not three gods but one God, who has the same and equal influence, authority, power, and glory. God the Father plans and rules all creation, the Son of God works out salvation of human beings, and God the Holy Spirit helps God the Father and God the Son of God work out salvation of human beings."

Strictly speaking, however, this answer is not totally in accordance with the Bible (Matt. 24:36; John 14:28; 1 Cor. 3:23; Acts 1:7; Col. 1:15, etc.). Therefore, the trinity theory shall be fully demonstrated based on the Bible only in the future.

Christianity is not polytheism nor henotheism but a faith in the one and only God. Henotheism says there are many gods and there is the greatest supreme god. A faith in the one and only God says that there are no other gods besides the one and only God of heaven and earth. Christianity is also not pantheism or polytheism but monotheism since it propagates that God Jehovah is the one and only God.

There are not many Bible verses in which Jesus Christ is directly mentioned as God. Isaiah 9:6 and John's Gospel 1:1 speak of "the word is God," in which the word is referred to as Jesus Christ. In John 20:28, Thomas says, "My Lord and my God." Romans 9:5 states, "Whose are the fathers, and of whom as concerning the flesh Christ came, who is over all, God blessed for ever. Amen." And 1 John 5:20 says, "And we know that the Son of God is come, and hath given us an understanding, that we may know him that is true, and we are in him that is true, even in his Son Jesus Christ. This is the true God, and eternal life." Moreover, in John 20:31, the apostle says, "But these are written, that ye might believe that Jesus is the Christ, the Son of God; and that believing ye might have life through his name," emphasizing that Jesus the Son of God the Savior. Romans 9:5 says, "Of whom are the fathers and from whom, according to the flesh, Christ came, who is over all, the eternally blessed God. Amen" (NJKV), which indicates that Jesus is God the Father. First Peter 1:3, says, "Blessed be the God and Father of our Lord Jesus Christ." There are many Bible verses in which God the Father says that "I myself am God and Jehovah" (Isa. 44:6, 43:12, etc.), but there is no verse in which Jesus says that "I myself am God" (see John 10:30, 33, 36, 17:11). *One* (ἑν in Greek, a neutral noun pointing to one nature or essence) is used in John 10:30, where Jesus says, "I and my Father are one."

Titus 2:13 records, "Looking for that blessed hope, and the glorious appearing of the great God and our Saviour Jesus Christ." The great God refers to Jehovah (see Deuteronomy 10:17 and Nehemiah 1:5). There is no such explicit expression as trinity in the Bible but just implicit ones such as 1 John 5:8-9: "For there are three that bear record in heaven, the Father, the Word, and the Holy Ghost: and these three are one. And there are three that bear witness in earth, the Spirit, and the water, and the blood: and these three agree in one."

Jesus the Son of God begins his existence in eternity (John 8:42; 1 Cor. 1:30; Col. 1:15) while God the Father is self-existing in eternity. The Shorter Catechism of Westminster asks, "Who is God?" The answer is, "God is a Spirit, which is self-existing; infinite in His wisdom, power, holiness, righteousness, goodness and truth; eternal; and unchanging." To God, there is no past, present, or future. To God, there is only everlasting present. The present is changeable but eternity is not. His eternity does not mean His timelessness but aseity, which human beings cannot fully understand.

The term *Jehovah* (Lord) is always expressed in the singular form while *Elohim* (God) is the singular of the plural form of El. Jehovah, God's official designation. He begets Jesus Christ His only son (John 8:58, 17:5, 24; Acts 13:33; Col. 1:15) and the Holy Spirit comes to exist at a certain point of time. "But of him are ye in Christ Jesus, who of God is made unto us wisdom, and righteousness, and sanctification, and redemption" (1 Cor. 1:30; Col. 1:15). "Who is the image of the invisible God, the firstborn of every creature" (Col. 1:15). "Christ Jesus is the firstborn of every creature" implies that Jesus Christ the Son of God is dependent on God the Father for the form of His existence (1 Cor. 15:28, 3:23). And Romans 8:29 and Hebrews 1:6 say that Jesus Christ the Son of God is the firstborn among many brethren. It implies that not all of God the Father, the Son of God and the Holy Spirit are self-existing but only Jehovah God the Father is (Exod. 3:14). Jehovah God the Father does not have a starting point for His existence while Jesus Christ, God's only-begotten son, does. Psalms 2:7 records, "the LORD hath said unto me, Thou art my Son; this day have I begotten thee."

"Behold my servant, whom I uphold; mine elect, in whom my soul delighteth; I have put my spirit upon him: he shall bring forth judgment to the Gentiles" (Isa. 42:1). This verse implies that God put His spirit upon Jesus at a certain point in time before the beginning, when God created the heaven and the earth.

"The LORD possessed me in the beginning of his way, before his works of old. I was set up from everlasting, from the beginning, or ever the earth was" (Prov. 8:22-23). "And now, O Father, glorify thou me with thine own self with the glory which I had with thee before the world was" (John 17:5). According to the Bible, before the beginning, Jesus the Son of God is begotten by Jehovah God and starts to exist (preexistence, John 17:5) in eternity before all creatures (; Ps. 89:27; Rom. 8:29; Col. 1:15). After that, angels or spiritual beings came into being. Then, some angels became corrupt and changed into evil spirits.

Jesus asked His disciples, "Whom say ye that I am?" Peter answered, "Thou art the Christ, the Son of the living God" (Matt. 16:16). Jesus was very pleased and said, "That thou art Peter, and upon this rock I will build my church; and the gates of hell shall not prevail against it." (Matt. 16:18). Here, Jesus clearly and correctly clarified His identity as the Son of God (the only-begotten son).

In John's Gospel, in order to keep His disciples from being afraid of His going to God the Father, Jesus says "I will not leave you comfortless: I will come to you." He also says, "I will pray the Father, and he shall give you another Comforter, that he may abide with you for ever. Even the Spirit of truth; whom the world cannot receive, because it seeth him not, neither knoweth him: but ye know him; for he dwelleth with you, and shall be in you" (John 14:16-17).

The Holy Spirit is a Comforter and the Spirit of truth. *Comforter* is also translated as helper (NBU), protector (M.E.B), counselor (RSV and NIV), advocate (N.E.B), and friend (Message). Isaiah 9:6 says that Jesus shall be called Wonderful (אלפ in Hebrew, meaning, wonder of a counselor; see Isa. 11:1-2), Counsellor (יעץ in Hebrew and παρακλητος in Greek; meaning, the original counselor). There are one Comforter and another Comforter. The two Comforters have the same nature and function. First John 2:1 records, "We have an advocate with the Father, Jesus Christ the righteous." According to the original Greek language, the advocate in this verse is the above-said comforter.

To sum up, our Lord Jesus Christ is God's only-begotten son, the Savior (Matt. 16:16; John 1:41), a Comforter (1 John 2:1), one proceeding from God the Father before all was created (Acts 13:33; 1 Cor. 1:30; Col. 1:15), one who was with God the Father in the beginning when God created all creation (John 1:2), smaller than God the Father (John 14:28), and one who shall take the book out of the right hand of him that sits upon the white throne (Rev. 5:7).

God the Father has made the Jesus both Lord and Christ (Acts 2:36) and given all power to Jesus (Matt. 28:18). And God the Father has sealed Jesus Christ (John 6:27), which implies that Jesus is a possession of God the Father. "But of that day and hour knoweth no man, no, not the angels of heaven, but my Father only" (Matt. 24:36), implies that Jesus Christ the Son of God is not Jehovah God the Father, who is omniscient, omnipotent and absolute (John 14:28; Mark 13:32; Matt. 24:36). Jesus is not self-existing (John 8:42; Col. 1:15) nor everlasting. Only God the Father is everlasting, self-existing, and absolute. Therefore, Jehovah is the one and only God the Father.

Jesus the Son of God makes a prayer to God the Father and does nothing of Himself but, as the Father hath taught Him, He speaks things. "Jesus said unto them, If God were your Father, ye would love me: for I proceeded forth and came from God; neither came I of myself, but he sent me" (John 8:42). "Who is the image of the invisible God, the firstborn of every creature" (Col. 1:15). "And ye are Christ's; and Christ is God's" (1 Cor. 3:23; John 6:27). "The head of Christ is God" (1 Cor. 11:3). "The LORD is God, and that there is none else" (1 Kings 8:60; Deut. 4:35,39). First Corinthians 8:5-6 records, "For though there be that are called gods, whether in heaven or in earth (as there be gods many, and lords many). But to us there is but one God, the Father, of whom are all things, and we in him; and one Lord Jesus Christ, by whom are all things, and we by him." "Thus saith the LORD the King of Israel, and his redeemer the LORD of hosts; I am the first, and I am the last; and beside me there is no God" (Isa. 44:6). "But the LORD is the true God, he is the living God, and an everlasting king" (Jer. 10:10). Still, our Lord Jesus Christ is God (Eph. 1:3).

The relationship between God the Father and Jesus Christ the Son of God is clearly shown in this verse: "But to us there is but one God, the Father, of whom are all things, and we in him; and one Lord Jesus Christ, by whom are all things, and we by him" (1 Cor. 8:6), which is called a contrasting Bible verse by polytheists and monotheists. In this verse, "we by him" implies that we were also created in the beginning by God the Father and Jesus Christ. And 1 Corinthians 15:28 records, "And when all things shall be subdued unto him, then shall the Son also himself be subject unto him that put all things under him, that God may be all in all." "Then cometh the end, when he shall have delivered up the kingdom to God, even the Father; when he shall have put down all rule and all authority and power" (1 Cor. 15:24), which implies that Jesus the Son of God will submit to God the Father. Therefore, it is indicated that Jesus the Son of God does not have the same authority, power, influence, self-existence and absolute power as Jehovah God the Father (John 5:30, 8:26, 42, 16:28; Phil. 3:21) and that the two are not one. God the Father is not a Comforter like Jesus Christ or the Holy Spirit is (1 John 2:1; John 14:16), nor a mediator between men and God, like Jesus the Son of God (1 Tim. 2:5), nor the firstborn among many brethren (Rom. 8:29), but the only Lord of all, the God and Lord of Jesus Christ (Mark 12:29) and the head of Jesus Christ (1 Cor. 11:3).

People may say that as a son of a man is a man, and the young of a bear is a bear, so the son of God is a God. Never! Because the Bible repeatedly stresses that there is only one God. Only one God is enough since Jehovah God the Father is living forever and has everlasting power, authority and glory, and He does not need to have a successor. It is why Jesus the Son of God says, "The first of all the commandments is, Hear, O Israel; The Lord our God is one Lord" (Mark 12:29). In this verse, Jesus does not call the Lord "your God" but "our God," which implies that God the Father or Jehovah is the God of Jesus himself and only Lord. "We have one Father, even God" (John 8:41, 17:3). Here, *only* means not "one" but "absolute." As Jesus the only-begotten son exists, so does the one and only God.

No Bible verse records that Jesus Christ is the only God. In the Bible, Zechariah 4 and Revelation 11 mention olive trees and candlesticks. What do they mean? Candlesticks (Exod. 25:31-40, 37:17-24) may be regarded as a symbol of the tabernacle or church; they give light when their lamps are supplied with oil from olive trees (Zech. 4:2-3, 12). Zechariah 4:11-12 gives the meaning of the two olive trees, "These are the two anointed ones, that stand by the LORD of the whole earth" (see Rev. 11:4-5, 11-12, 1:12-20). The anointed one is Messiah (the original form is משיח; Ps. 2:2), which is חיש in Hebrew and χριστός (Christ, John 1:41) in Greek and means the savior. Samaritans called Messiah Taheb (one who is to come again; Jer. 23:5, Zech. 3:8, John 4:25.)

The word *Messiah* is derived from Isaiah 61:1, which reads, "The Spirit of the Lord GOD is upon me; because the LORD hath anointed me to preach good tidings unto the meek; he hath sent me to bind up the brokenhearted, to proclaim liberty to the captives, and the opening of the prison to them that are bound." Jehovah God anoints Jesus and consecrates Him as the Messiah (Ps. 45:7; Isa. 28:16; Heb. 1:9). "God hath made the same Jesus, whom ye have crucified, both Lord and Christ" (Acts 2:36). Then who is the anointed one? That the anointed one is Jesus Christ is clearly stated in Daniel 9:24-26, Isaiah 61:1, 42:1-4, Psalms 45:7. Acts 4:27 states, "For of a truth against thy holy child Jesus, whom thou hast anointed." Psalms 2:7 clearly records, "The LORD hath said unto me, Thou art my Son; this day have I begotten thee," which also implies that the anointed one is Jesus Christ. Jesus sits on the right hand of God (Mark 16:19, 22:44; Acts 7:55; Rom. 8:34; Eph. 1:20; 1 Pet. 3:22) and "stands by the LORD of the whole earth" (Zech. 4:14). Also, "As for me, this is my covenant with them, saith the LORD; My spirit that is upon thee, and my words which I have put in thy mouth, shall not depart out of thy mouth, nor out of the mouth of thy seed, nor out of the mouth of thy seed's seed, saith the LORD, from henceforth and for ever" (Isa. 59:21). Therefore, "the two anointed ones (משׁיח in Hebrew, meaning 'sons of the oil'), that stand by the LORD of the whole earth" in Zechariah 4:14 are the two comforters: Jesus Christ the Son of God (1 John 2:1) and the Holy Spirit (John 14:16).

To sum up, the two Comforters, Jesus Christ the Son of God on the right and the Holy Spirit of truth on the left, have always been with God the Father since He created all things (Gen. 1:26; John 1:3; Prov. 8:22-31, etc.) and will be everlastingly with God to the last moment of the history.

Lastly, I want to touch on ancient Christology presented by Arius (250-336). He contends that the Holy Spirit and Christ's Spirit dwell in us, but God the Father does not. Unlike in the case of general Christians who are God's foster sons (Rom. 8:15; Gal. 3:26), God the Father always dwells in the Son of God (2 Cor. 5:19), who is God's only-begotten son since the Father and the Son are one essence. As He says, "I am not alone, because the Father is with me" (John 8:16, 29, 16:32; Acts 10:38). God the Father always dwells in Jesus so that Jesus may be Immanuel (Isa. 7:14), that he may be called God, praised, and worshiped. "That all men should honour the Son, even as they honour the Father. He that honoureth not the Son honoureth not the Father which hath sent him" (John 5:23). Colossians 1:15 denies the trinity since it says that Jesus is the image of the invisible God and the firstborn of every creature. Jesus the Son of God is begotten by God the Father.   So there was a time when Jesus the Son of God did not exist. It implies that Jesus the Son of God is not everlasting. At a time point before all things were created, the Son of God was born and began to be with God the Father. After being resurrected, Jesus ascended to heaven and has sat on the right of God (Mark 16:19; Heb. 1:3; Acts 7:55, etc.) but He will be with us in the form of

Comforter the Holy Spirit (Rom. 8:9) till the end of this world (Matt. 28:20).

Origen calls the Christology of Arius the theory of subordination. What is difference between Comforter Jesus Christ the Son of God (1 John 2:1) and Comforter the Holy Spirit of truth? Both are comforters, but Jesus is distinguished from the Holy Spirit since Jesus was once incarnated while the Holy Spirit remains a spiritual being. Jesus Christ, God's only-begotten son, appeared in the form of a human being, worked out the salvation of men, and will come again in a resurrection body. Jesus is the only mediator between Jehovah God and men (1 Tim. 2:5) and serves as a "ladder" (Gen. 28:12) between God the Father and human beings. The Spirit also helps our infirmities: for we know not what we should pray for as we ought: but the Spirit itself makes intercession for us with groaning which cannot be uttered (Rom. 8:26).

There is no expression of the Holy Spirit in the Old Testament. "His Holy Spirit," used in Isaiah 63:10-11, is the Spirit of God. In the Old Testament, there appear such expressions as the Spirit of God (Gen. 1:2, etc.), the Spirit of Jehovah or LORD (1 Sam. 16:13), or your (thy) Spirit (Ps. 104:30). The Holy Spirit can be found in the New Testament only, as can be Jesus the only begotten son of God (see John 14:16, Acts 1:4,5). As Jesus the Son of God came first into this earth in the New Testament times (4 BC), so the Holy Spirit came first into this earth and always resides here (John 14:16). The Holy Spirit is one of the two Comforters (John 14:16, 1 John 2:1).

The Holy Spirit is not God's only-begotten son nor was incarnated but He helps work out the salvation of men till the end of the world. Jesus and the Holy Spirit are both Comforters, but they are different from each other because Jesus is God's only-begotten son (John 14:16; 1 John 2:1) while the Holy

Spirit is the spirit of truth (John 14:26). There is no Bible verse that directly indicates that the Holy Spirit is God, except for Acts 5:3-4, which record, "But Peter said, Ananias, why hath Satan filled thine heart to lie to the Holy Ghost, and to keep back part of the price of the land?... Thou hast not lied unto men, but unto God." These verses indicate that lying to the Holy Ghost is equal to lying to God (also see 1 John 5:8). It is a distorted suggestion that the Holy Spirit is correspondent in the Old Testament with such expressions as the Spirit of God, the Spirit of Jehovah, My Spirit, and so forth. It is not different from an assertion that Jesus is the Holy Spirit or vice versa. The only-begotten Son of God is Jesus. In the New Testament as well, there is clear discrimination among the Spirit of God, the Spirit of Jesus, and the Holy Spirit. Some contend that God the Father was active in the Old Testament age, the Son of God was in the New Testament age, and the Holy Spirit is after the Pentecostal. However, the triune God is active in every age. In the Old Testament age, God is active for us; in the New Testament age, God is with us; and in the Holy Spirit age, God is still in the saints.

The Doctrine of God

Human beings can not comprehend God the Creator, but we can conceive of and conjecture about Him. We can know God when we read the Bible. A core reason to know the doctrine of God is that it leads us to our salvation. When we know and believe in God in a right manner, we establish right relationship with God and serve Him in a right way. In 1 Chronicles 28:9, King David left a will saying, "And thou, Solomon my son, know thou the God of thy father, and serve him with a perfect heart and with a willing mind: for the LORD searcheth all hearts, and understandeth all the imaginations of the thoughts: if thou seek him, he will be found of thee; but if thou forsake him, he will cast thee off for ever." In his will, David asked his beloved son Solomon to know and serve God rightly. "Come, and let us return unto the LORD: for he hath torn, and he will heal us; he hath smitten, and he will bind us up. After two days will he revive us: in the third day he will raise us up, and we shall live in his sight. Then shall we know, if we follow on to know the LORD: his going forth is prepared as the morning; and he shall come unto us as the rain, as the latter and former rain unto the earth" (Hos. 6:1-3).

Being a God requires a number of qualifications including a power to create things, a power to control and rule all creation (Exod. 19:5; Deut. 32:39; 1 Sam. 2:6-7; 1 Chr. 16;31, 29:12; Ps. 93:1), and while the doctrine of God comprises many aspects, I would like to briefly look at three of God's attributes: eternity, absolutism and ubiquity.

(1) Eternity

Everlasting is different from permanent, which also refers to continuing forever from the present. In contrast, everlasting refers to something without beginning (alpha) or end (omega), like a circle.

Eternity is not created or born but self-existing. Without self-existence, eternity cannot be realized. "God hath fulfilled the same unto us their children, in that he hath raised up Jesus again; as it is also written in the second psalm, Thou art my Son, this day have I begotten thee" (Acts 13:33). "Who is the image of the invisible God, the firstborn of every creature" (Col. 1:15). Jesus is God's only son and was begotten (Prov. 8:22-24; John 8:23, 16:28; Acts 13:33; Col. 1:15) by God and has been everlasting since then. God's unicity is dependent on self-existence and eternity. Human beings belong to the material world and have a past, present, and future. In contrast, Jehovah God exists timelessly and is always and eternally present, without beginning or end, past or future. Jesus the Son of God was born in the past (in the beginning before all creation was created) (Prov. 8:22-31, etc.).

(2) Absolutism

Absolutism implies that God is omniscient and omnipotent. Jesus says in Matthew 24:36, "But of that day and hour knoweth no man, no, not the angels of heaven, but my Father only." Does Jesus tell a lie when He says that? Also, Acts 1:7 says, "And he said unto them, It is not for you to know the times or the seasons, which the Father hath put in his own power." The Bible says that only Jehovah God the Father knows everything in heaven and earth, and only Jehovah is the Almighty God. Jesus, the Son of God, is not the Almighty but the Mighty (רידא in Hebrew; 'strong' in the Message Bible) God, considering these verses: Genesis 17:1 ("I am the Almighty God"), Isaiah 9:6 ("For unto us a child is born, unto us a son is given: and the government shall be upon his shoulder: and his name shall be called Wonderful, Counsellor, The mighty God, The everlasting Father, The Prince of Peace.") and others.

(3) Ubiquity

Ubiquity refers to God's omnipresence, which is different from immensity. *Immense* suggests that God surpasses all space and time that He is not limited in but infinitely fills with His realities.

For example, assuming that the universe is as big as a bead, which is placed at the hand of God, the universe is in God's hand, and so are the earth, sun, moon and stars. Then, immense God fills every corner of the universe. God is not limited to time and space because He is a spirit without a body (John 4:24). The ubiquitous God exists in each corner of all spaces and dwells in every place. The immense God leads to transcendent God and ubiquitous God to immanent God, who is everlasting, absolute, and ubiquitous.

Unlike dualism, pluralism, polytheism, pantheism, or henotheism, monotheism contends that God is the one and only. Christianity is monotheistic. One may wonder how God can be present in each and every corner of this world at the same time. But He can, and it is paradoxically true (i.e., oxymoron). Let me say something of the omnipresence of God.

They say that the speediest in this world is light, which revolves 7.5 times around the earth in a second. But there something speedier than light: thinking. In thinking, there is no concept of distance, since thinking can reach anywhere in no time. In the spiritual realm, the speed of thinking or imagination is applicable. The spiritual realm does not contain concepts of time and distance like in the material world. Nor does the spiritual realm need any means of transportation or communication because there is no distance, and any thinking can be understood instantly and automatically if required. In such a nonmaterial world, God transcends the speed of thinking because even thinking is not necessary to God.

God sees through the thinking of all human beings. Even before I think of something, God sees through and knows my mind because God is omniscient and omnipotent. To speak more specifically, God goes from His throne and comes to us so quickly and permanently that we feel that He is always with us. And God sends us sunlight so continually that we feel it always around us even though it is reaching us at intervals.

The absolute omnipotent omnipresence of God implies that He is not only in each corner of the universe but in Hades as well. God is immensely omnipresent in the universe.

To sum up, God is the one and only being not only in heaven but also on the earth. Creatures cannot fully know God their Creator but can only understand Him as far the Bible reveals Him.

In the Old Testament, there are many names for God. The most familiar are:

(1) EL SHADAI (Almighty God)—Gen. 17:1

(2) JIREH (God our provider)—Gen. 22:14

(3) M'KADESH (God our sanctifier)—Lev. 20:8

(4) NISSI (God our banner or flag)—Exo. 17:15

(5) RAPHA (God our healer)—Exo. 15:26

(6) ROHI (Lord our shepherd)—Ps. 23:31

(7) SHALOM (Lord our peace)—Jud. 6:24

(8) SABBAOTH (Lord our hosts)—1 Sam. 1:3

(9) TSDKENU (God our righteousness)—Jer. 23:6

(10) ADONAI (Lord or Master)—Ps. 69:6

(11) ELOHIM (God our creator)—Gen. 1:1

(12) JEHOVAH (eternal God)—Exo. 3:14

Of these, three are representative:

Creator - םיהולא (Elohim) in Hebrew

Our Lord or the Lord - ינודא (Adonai) in Hebrew

Everlasting God - הוהי (Jehovah) in Hebrew

Now, let me explain about *Elohim*. In the Hebrew Old Testament, the universe is referred to as "heaven and earth." Without exception, *heaven* is expressed in the plural, "heavens" (םע) about 420 times (Deut. 10:14; 1 Kings 8:27; 2 Chr. 2:6; Neh. 9:6, and others). This is because there is the atmospheric layer, where birds fly and clouds travel, and another layer, space, where there is no air but stars and the Milky Way. In Hebrew, *the earth* (הארץ) is expressed in the singular form. The term *create* is also expressed in the singular form (אורבל).

A Hebrew sentence must have one subject and one verb. If the subject *Elohim* has the singular form of verb *create*, the creator is the one and only God. However, if the subject *Elohim* has the plural form of verb *create*, then the creator refers to alien gods, rulers, judges, angels or others.

The six-day creation by God is described in Genesis 1:26-28. "And God said, Let us make man in our image, after our likeness: and let them have dominion over the fish of the sea, and over the fowl of the air, and over the cattle, and over all the earth, and over every creeping thing that creepeth upon the earth. So God created man in his own image, in the image of God created he him; male and female created he them. And God blessed them, and God said unto them, Be fruitful, and multiply, and replenish the earth, and subdue it: and have dominion over the fish of the sea, and over the fowl of the air, and over every living thing that moveth upon the earth." This report is a very detailed description of the creation of human beings and clearly says that they were created from nothing.

In the description, *Adam* has two meanings: a common man and the husband of Eve. God made man in His image and after His likeness. What is God's image (εικονα in Greek and צלם in Hebrew) and likeness (ομοιωμα in Greek and ויןמד in Hebrew)? According to the meaning of the prepositions *in* and *after* used in this sentence, it implies that man was made against the image of God and like the appearance of God. Likeness means external shape or appearance while image means inner nature. God's corporality is not of fish, elephants, or the like but of a man who resembles God or Jesus (Dan. 7:9; John 14:9;

Rev. 1:14). A man's shape was the same as he is today, when he was initially created. When he was depraved, he did not lose his external appearance but his inner quality of God's image, not His corporality but incorporality comprising reason, sentiment, and conscience.

Since Adam and Eve ate the fruit of the tree of knowledge and sinned, their consciences were seared with a hot iron, becoming totally depraved and disabled. Committing the original sin, immediately Adam lost God's image in him and came to have a depraved nature. Since then, all human beings with such a depraved nature came to have been sentenced to death under sin (Rom. 5:12). In the East, Mencius (372-289 BC) advocates the theory that human nature is fundamentally good while Xunzi (340-245 BC) maintains the theory that human nature is fundamentally evil. Both theories make sense. The former refers to men's original nature while the latter to the nature of men who have taken the fruit of the tree of knowledge and became depraved (Gen. 8:21). Genesis 1:27 says that God created man in his own image and in the image of God; male and female created He them.

"And God said unto them, Be fruitful, and multiply, and replenish the earth, and subdue it: and have dominion over the fish of the sea, and over the fowl of the air, and over every living thing that moveth upon the earth" (Gen. 1:28). They were not commanded to live in a limited area but permitted to stay in any corner around the world they wanted. Chapter 1 of Genesis clearly says that the first man and woman were created from nothing, and Genesis 2:7 tells that God formed man (Adam, the husband of Eve) of the dust of the ground. "And the LORD God formed man of the dust of the ground, and breathed into his nostrils the breath of life; and man became a living soul." "And the LORD God planted a garden eastward in

Eden; and there he put the man whom he had formed" (Gen. 2:8).

In Chapters 1 and 2 of Genesis, 4 kinds of Hebrew word are used to represent producing:

- In His Hebrew designation, God (Elohim) in Genesis 2:7 is different from God (Jehovah) in Genesis 1:27. Elohim is the majestic plural form of *eloahh* (Exod. 12:12; Deut. 32:15), whose root is *Ala* (meaning "vowing"). A majestic plural or singular form was a rhetoric used in the ancient Near East and even in ancient Korea to emphasize or specially represent the authority, majesty, or importance of someone. Therefore, Elohim is singular and stands for the one and only God because it is used along with the singular form of verb. In Genesis 1:1 of the Septuagint, Elohim is presented in the singular, not plural. Elohim presented in the plural form does not mean that God is plural.

Someone contends that Elohim in the plural form refers to the trinity of God: the Father, the Son of God, and the Holy Spirit. This is not true, either. In the Septuagint, God the Father only is represented in the singular form. "Thus saith the LORD, thy redeemer, and he that formed thee from the womb, I am the LORD that maketh all things; that stretcheth forth the heavens alone; that spreadeth abroad the earth by myself" (Isa. 44:24). And Isaiah 44:8 records, "Is there a God beside me? yea, there is no God; I know not any." Some assert that Elohim is the plural form of El, which usually stands for God and from which are derived *elim* and *eloah*. In the Bible, elohim represented in the proper noun always refers to God the Father. In contrast, *elohim* represented in a common term refers to alien gods (Gen. 31:30; Judg. 2:12, 5:8; Deut. 32:17; Exod. 7:1; 1 Cor. 8:5, etc.), angels (Ps. 8:5, etc.), judges (Exod.

21:6, etc.) or others. Exodus 7:1 records, "And the LORD said unto Moses, See, I have made thee a god to Pharaoh: and Aaron thy brother shall be thy prophet." Moses was also considered elohim (a god) by Pharaoh.

Psalms 82:6 records, "I have said, Ye are gods [elohim]; and all of you are children of the most High" (see John 10:34). Jehovah refers to God the Father only. But elohim does not. It is used in the Bible 4,370 times and 2,250 times in the Old Testament including Genesis 1:1 and Chapters 2 and 3 of Genesis. Elohim represents God our Creator; great, strong and powerful God, or God of holy glory, who men cannot easily approach. Jehovah (Yehoah, Jahweh or Yahweh) is a noun represented in the Hebrew singular form, and Jehovah and Adonai are translated into the Lord. The four letters (יהוה in Hebrew and YHVH in English) of the tetragrammaton are softly sounded Jehovah according to the masoretic text and some scholars read it as Yahweh, which is commonly used by Old Testament scholars but has not been fully proved to the scholars in general.

Jehovah is mentioned in the Bible 6,820 times and 5,321 times in the Old Testament including Genesis 4:1-16. English versions of the Bible seldom mention Jehovah. Most of them have Lord or God instead of Jehovah. Jehovah means eternal God, the source of all things, the alpha and the omega, the beginning and the end, the first and the last. Jehovah is the only proper name of God given by Himself. Jehovah, which originates from *ehyeh* in Hebrew, means I AM THAT I AM, which refers to self-existing God, in Exodus 3:14. Jehovah is the singular form of a proper noun representing God the Father, who is the only eternal and absolute God and differentiated from Jesus the Son of God or the Holy Spirit, who is not self-existing

(Col. 1:15; 1 Cor. 1:30; John 8:42; Prov. 8:22-23, etc.). Jehovah is translated into the Lord in the Septuagint.

The term *Lord* is differently applied than Jehovah depending on whether it is used in a religious or non-religious way. It may be applied to God the Father or Jesus and represent a secular lord or a legal influence or authority. In an English version, Jehovah is translated into the LORD while Adonai into the Lord, which may refer to Jesus, or into a lord which refers to a secular master (Matt. 24:48,). In the Message, Jesus Christ is never expressed as Lord but as Master (John 20:28). Isaiah 61:1 records, "The Spirit of the Lord GOD is upon me; because the LORD hath anointed me." The Spirit of the Lord GOD is translated from the Hebrew original חור ינודא 'הוהי (Jehovah Adonai Ruah). It implies that not Adonai but Jehovah is the only proper noun referring to God the Father. First Corinthians 8:6 records, "But to us there is but one God, the Father, of whom are all things, and we in him; and one Lord Jesus Christ, by whom are all things, and we by him."

In this verse, God the Father is designated as God while Jesus Christ the Son as Lord. In the New Testament, *lord* is applied to a master of servants (1 Corinthians 8:5; Matt. 25:18) or to an emperor, in the same manner as *elohim* is used as a proper noun (representing God) or as a common noun (representing a god). Therefore, it is wrong that Jehovah is confused with other expressions like Adonai. People would not use the word Jehovah but to replace it with other expressions since God commands that thou shalt not take the name of the LORD thy God in vain (Exod. 20:7). However, it is not a good practice. For example, the word (פתיחה) representing the beginning in Genesis 1:1 of a Hebrew version means a different thing from the corresponding word (αρχή) in the Septuagint: the former stands for a time point when human time and space were begun while the latter stands for eternity before the beginning. It calls for careful researches into the original languages of the Bible.

As the official name of the Son of God is Christ and His personal name is Jesus, so Jehovah is the only personal proper name of God the Father. Therefore, Jesus is the Son of God, not the Holy Spirit or God the Father; and God the Father is not Jesus since Jehovah is self-existing (Exod. 3:14) and the only God the Father. Isaiah 42:8 records, "I am the LORD: that is my name." Exodus 3:15 records, "And God said moreover unto Moses, Thus shalt thou say unto the children of Israel, the LORD God of your fathers, the God of Abraham, the God of Isaac, and the God of Jacob, hath sent me unto you: this is my name for ever, and this is my memorial unto all generations." And "Even the LORD God of hosts; the LORD is his memorial" (Ho. 12:5). So God is the official designation of God the Father and Jehovah is a proper noun representing the personal proper name of God the Father.

Exodus 6:3 records, "And I appeared unto Abraham, unto Isaac, and unto Jacob, by the name of God Almighty, but by my name JEHOVAH was I not known to them." Jehovah is loving God since He is so benign as to make coats of skins and clothed Adam and Eve in Chapter 3 of Genesis, so considerate of Cain when he is a fugitive and vagabond in the earth so as set a mark upon Cain lest any finding him should kill him in Chapter 4 of Genesis, so careful of men as to dwell in us not due to our merits but to His graces for the purpose of helping, protecting, guiding and blessing them.

That God is love (1 John 4:8, 16) is demonstrated by the fact that God loves human beings who are sinners and His foster sons (Rom. 8:15; Gal. 4:5) so much that He let crucified His only-begotten son Jesus, who said seven words on the cross

(Matt. 27:46; Mark 15:34; Luke 23:34, 43, 46; John 19:26, 28, 30). On the cross, "Jesus cried with a loud voice, saying, Eloi, Eloi, lama sabachthani? which is, being interpreted, My God, my God, why hast thou forsaken me?" (Mark 15:34). These words are cited in the Aramaic language from Psalms 22:1 in Hebrew: *eloi* means "my God," *lama* means "why," and *sabachthani* means "forsaken." It may be paraphrased, ''My own father, why do you forsake me your own son and love human beings who are your foster sons more than me to let me who am your only-begotten son crucified?" God loves men so much as to leave His only-begotten son to die.

What is the difference in meaning between Jehovah God in the singular form and Elohim God in the plural form attested in Genesis 2:7? There is not so much difference between them as between Jehovah and Elohim. Deuteronomy 6:4 records, "Hear, O Israel: The LORD our God is one LORD." In this verse, *one* is in the compound singular form, which is a little different from the absolute singular form. The God who controls, takes care of and kindly looks after men is Jehovah God expressed in the singular or plural form in Genesis 2:7, Genesis 3:21, Exodus 6:7, Deuteronomy 4:7, Deuteronomy 6:4-5, Joshua 8:30, and so forth.

Creationism

Now, let me briefly tell about the creation story recorded in Genesis 1. The purpose of God's creation of all creatures is clearly stated in "Even every one that is called by my name: for I have created him for my glory, I have formed him; yea, I have made him" (Isa. 43:7). In the everlasting spiritual realm, Jehovah God the Creator created time (χρόνος) and space as today out of nothing in the beginning. That time was created means that there was a point when time was started, and it implies that there will be an end of this world. The beginning was not included in the first of six יום‎s (Gen. 1:5). In other words, the heaven and the earth were created out of naught in the beginning before יום‎ 1. After the heaven and the earth were created, יום‎ 1 came into being and the light was divided from the darkness.

After the beginning, there came into being יום‎s. After the universe and the earth were created from nothing, God said (λεματι in Greek and רמוא‎ in Hebrew), "Let there be" and there was יום‎ 1 started, not created (Gen. 1:5). It means that the beginning was not created on יום‎ 1. "Creation from nothing" is different from "coming into being according to God's word." In Genesis 1, God the Creator ordered that something should come into being upon God's permission. In Genesis 1:1 and 2, heaven and earth did not come into being according to God's word but were created by God. "In the beginning God created the heaven and the earth" (Gen. 1:1). This creation was not newly made with something like soil or ribs but made out of nothing with just with words (Gen. 1:27) or hands (Ps. 8:3; Isa. 44:24, 45:12). Therefore, this creation is applicable to Jehovah God the Creator only.

Concerning this creation, Isaiah 44:24 records, "Thus saith the LORD, thy redeemer, and he that formed thee from the womb, I am the LORD that maketh all things; that stretcheth forth the heavens alone; that spreadeth abroad the earth by myself." And Isaiah 45:12 records, "I have made the earth, and created man upon it: I, even my hands, have stretched out the heavens, and all their host have I commanded." Psalms 8:3 records, "When I consider thy heavens, the work of thy fingers, the moon and the stars, which thou hast ordained" ("your handmade sky-jewelry, moon and stars mounted in their settings," Message). "Even every one that is called by my name:

for I have created him for my glory, I have formed him; yea, I have made him" (Isa. 43:7). "Where wast thou when I laid the foundations of the earth? Declare, if thou hast understanding. Who hath laid the measures thereof, if thou knowest? or who hath stretched the line upon it? Whereupon are the foundations thereof fastened? or who laid the corner stone thereof" (Job 38:4-6). Isaiah 48:13 records, "Mine hand also hath laid the foundation of the earth, and my right hand hath spanned the heavens: when I call unto them, they stand up together."

Proverbs 8:22-31 records, "The LORD possessed me in the beginning of his way, before his works of old. I was set up from everlasting, from the beginning, or ever the earth was. When there were no depths, I was brought forth; when there were no fountains abounding with water. Before the mountains were settled, before the hills was I brought forth: While as yet he had not made the earth, nor the fields, nor the highest part of the dust of the world. When he prepared the heavens, I was there: when he set a compass upon the face of the depth: When he established the clouds above: when he strengthened the fountains of the deep: When he gave to the sea his decree, that the waters should not pass his commandment: when he appointed the foundations of the earth: Then I was by him, as one brought up with him: and I was daily his delight, rejoicing always before him; Rejoicing in the habitable part of his earth; and my delights were with the sons of men."

These verses demonstrate that the heaven and the earth did not come into being by means of the word but were created. Some contend that all creation came into being by means of God's word, which is supported by such verses as Psalms 33:6: "By the word (רבד in Hebrew and "command" in the Message or NIV) of the LORD were the heavens made; and all the host of them by the breath of his mouth." Hebrew 11:3 says, "Through faith we understand that the worlds were framed by the word (fore reference, λόγος: word is different from ρημα: command) of God, so that things which are seen were not made of things which do appear." Second Peter 3:5 says, "For this they willingly are ignorant of, that by the word of God the heavens were of old, and the earth standing out of the water and in the water." They contend so because they are confused about the creation of the heaven and the earth recorded in Genesis 1:1-2 and the creation of מויהs in Genesis 1:3 and the following verses by means of God's word. Job, Isaiah, Psalms, Proverbs and other books demonstrate that the heaven and the earth were created before Genesis 1:3 and the following verses, where "God said" appears.

"Creating" the heaven and the earth as stated in Genesis 1:1 is the first of three times creating is mentioned in Chapter 1 of Genesis (Gen. 1:1, 21, 27). That is to say, creating the universe and the earth out of nothing was not accomplished by God's word as in the case of מויה 1 stated in Genesis 1:3 but was created (Job 38:4-6; Ps. 8:3, 104:5; Isa. 44:24, 45:12). Therefore, it is artificial, awkward, and strained from the standpoint of the words, sentences, and contexts to assume that what is stated in Genesis 1:1-2 is the same as what is stated in Genesis 1:3-5.

The universe and the earth were first created before the sun, the moon and the stars came into being (Gen. 1:14-19). It is in accordance with the statement, "And the earth was without form, and void; and darkness was upon the face of the deep. And the Spirit of God moved upon the face of the waters" (Gen. 1:2). The primitive earth created by God out of nothing was without form (in chaos) and void, and darkness was upon the face of the deep. This primitive earth was created before the other heavenly bodies like the sun, the moon and the stars, and it was unstable, fluid, without form and in darkness. No one knows how long such a primitive state lasted because the Bible says nothing about that. Some guess it lasted for billions of years.

It is correct and right to draw a reasonable conclusion about the creation history recorded in Genesis 1 after researching the descriptions in the relevant Bible verses and the objective facts compared and analyzed. The initial primitive earth was void, fluid, formless and shapeless (Gen. 1:2). After some prolonged time in such a state, God said and then six סויהs were created.

First day (סויה)

On סויה 1 in the beginning, God the Creator said, Let there be light: and there was light. This light came into being by means of God's word only, unlike the lights from the illuminators made with some materials on סויה four (Gen. 1:16). What are these lights? Or what kinds of light are they? The Bible says there are four kinds of light in this world:

(1) Lamplight, candle light, firewood light and others (Matt. 5:15)

(2) Lightening flash or electric light (1 Kings 18:38)

(3) Sunlight, star (a luminous body) light, moon (a reflector) light (1 Kings 20:11)

(4) Spiritual light or light of life (Job 3:20), light of the world (John 8:12), or Christian light (Matt. 5:14)

What of these four was made by God on סויה 1 stated in Genesis 1:3? The fourth light or the spiritual light was, since the others were not yet at that time (see the opinions of Augustine). What is the spiritual light? The Bible says that God and Jesus are lights which have existed before the creation of the world (1 John 1:5; James 1:17; John 8:12, 9:5) when the other lights than this spiritual light were not yet made in the natural world. So, according to the Bible, the light existing on סויה 1, when there were no visible luminous bodies (sun and stars, Gen. 1:15), is what makes the spiritual light come into being. All the visible and physical lights of the world were made on סויה 4 and later. Modern science has revealed that human bodies by themselves give off light (heat or energy), which cannot be sensed easily with the naked eye.

This implies that there are other lights that we can see with our naked eyes, in the same manner that there are other sounds than we can hear with our naked ears. Isaac Newton (1642-1727) says that all creatures including microorganisms have their colors, which are their lights. On סויה 1, God made such invisible lights in the primitive earth (Gen. 1:3). Second Corinthians 4:6 records, "For God, who commanded the light to shine out of darkness, hath shined in our hearts, to give the light of the knowledge of the glory of God in the face of Jesus Christ." "In him was life; and the life was the light of men" (John 1:4). "And the light shineth in darkness; and the darkness comprehended it not" (John 1:5). So, the light appearing on סויה 1 is not what was created (Gen. 1:14) but what makes the spiritual light come into being (Gen. 1:3). On סויה 4 (Gen. 1:14-15), there came into being the sun, moon, and stars (lighting units) to give light to the dark earth. Therefore, the lights appearing on סויה 4 are different from that on סוי 1 (Gen. 1:3) in their nature: the former is physical lights and the latter non-material light (John 8:12). The spiritual light was formed into being in the earth on סויה 1 by God's word. And God divided the light from the darkness. And God called the light 'day' (in which there is the spiritual light) and the darkness he called 'night' (in which there is the spiritual darkness, John 1:5).

There are spiritual day and night since Jesus says, "I must work the works of him that sent me, while it is day: the night cometh, when no man can work. As long as I am in the world, I am the light of the world" (John 9:4-5). The Apostle Paul says, "Ye are all the children of light, and the children of the day: we are not of the night, nor of darkness" (1 Thess. 5:5). It is why Christianity is also called the religion of light (Nestorianism). After creating the heaven and the earth in the beginning, God gave the spiritual light to this world. The sunlight and other physical lights including the day and the night were created on םויה 4 (Gen. 1:14) and later (Gen. 1:14-19). Then, what is םויה in the Hebrew language? First of all, all the םוי s stated in Genesis 1 do not have the definite article. םויה is counted in cardinal numbers, not in ordinal numbers (see the Message). םויה is mentioned in the Old Testament about 2,225 times and used in various ways. The following are the examples of the use of םויה.

(1) Day (day light, time or hour; Gen. 8:22)

(2) A day of 24 hours (all day, every day or full day; Gen. 39:10; Ps. 10:13)

(3) Now or a certain fixed day (a special day or scheduled day; Job 14:5-6; Exod. 6:28)

(4) Time (period or term; Gen. 2:4; 1 Sam. 1:21; Job 14:6; Ps. 90:4)

Therefore, םויה does not always mean a day of twenty-four hours. The exact meaning of םוי is dependent on the context. By the way, which of the above uses is applicable to the םויה first mentioned in Genesis 1:5? This is an important issue, concerning various theological theories that sharply confront each other. It is necessary to closely examine and analyze each and every word, verse, sentence, and relevant context of Chapter 1 of Genesis and then compare them with objective and general facts. First, a theological theory asserts that היום stated in Genesis 1 is a day of twenty-four hours, for the following reasons:

(1) היום means a day of 24 hours, a full day (Ps. 10:13) or day by day (Gen. 39:10).

(2) היום means a day since before יום is mentioned there is a statement "And the evening and the morning were the first day," which comprises twenty-four hours.

(3) After six היוםs, according to Genesis 2:2, God rested on the seventh day, which should also comprise twenty-four hours.

(4) God had completely created all creation in six היוםs or 144 hours.

Second, another theological theory maintains in the following manner: היום in Chapter 1 of Genesis does not mean a day of twenty-four hours but a certain period or time, for the following reasons:

(1) היום is not used as a day of twenty-four hours but as a certain season or period (Gen. 2:4; 1 Sam. 2:19).

(2) The earth started rotating on its axis and revolving around the sun only after the solar system was created.

(3) The evening and the morning came into being only after the sun was made. They came into being only on היום 4 stated in Genesis 1:14 or later times.

(4) The Bible says that היום (Gen. 1:5) is not a day since the sun, the moon, and the stars as well as days, months, years, and seasons were made on היום 4. In other words, because the word היום was used even before the concept and system of a day were set up, היום does not mean a day but a certain season or period.

(5) Before היום 4, the earth did not yet rotate on its axis nor revolved around the sun (since there was no sun) and there was no morning and evening. "And the evening and the morning were the first day" (Gen. 1:5) is a rhythmic expression for a poem. The reason why the evening is mentioned before the

morning may be due to expression practices of the original language of Hebrew or may be that the primitive earth had initially only darkness of the evening (Gen. 1:2).

(6) The light and darkness mentioned on סויה 1 are different from those on סוי 4, in which God the Creator initially created a rhythm of the cycle comprising four seasons.

Besides these, there are other theological theories, but I will skip them all here. Of all these, which is biblical? Let me return to the texts in Genesis 1. In order to know if סויה is used as a day, season or period, it is necessary to closely examine meaning, significance and content of each word regarding סויה 4 in Genesis 1:14-19, which says: "And God said, Let there be lights in the firmament of the heaven to divide the day from the night; and let them be for signs, and for seasons, and for days, and years: And let them be for lights in the firmament of the heaven to give light (ריאהל in Hebrew, Gen. 1:15,17) upon the earth: and it was so. And God made two great lights; the greater light to rule the day, and the lesser light to rule the night: he made the stars also. And God set them in the firmament of the heaven to give light upon the earth, and to rule over the day and over the night, and to divide the light from the darkness: and God saw that it was good. And the evening and the morning were the fourth day."

Here, according to the original language of the Bible, *lights* is plural and means the sun, the moon, and the stars including all the fixed stars, planets, and satellites in the universe. We must clearly understand that the *light* mentioned in Genesis 1:3 is light itself and *lights* in Genesis 1:14 are light-giving bodies. It means that illuminating bodies were first made on סויה 4. Moreover, light appearing on סויה 1 was not made with some materials but simply with God's word without any materials.

After God made lights (Gen. 1:16), day and night came into being to kick off the conception and system of a day of twenty-four hours. Another thing to note here is that the light and darkness divided in Genesis 1:4-5 are different in their nature from those in Genesis 1:18. It should not be accepted that the light and darkness divided in Genesis 1:4-5 is again divided in Genesis 1:18. Spiritual light was divided from darkness on יום 1 while visible physical light from darkness on יום 4. It is incongruous to contend that the happening on יום 1 was repeated on יום 4, since what happened on יום 1 is totally different from what happened on יום 4, in which God made lights (the sun, moon, and stars).

God did a different thing on each of the following יוםs. On יום 4, the identity of יום is very clearly revealed not as a day but as a season or period. God first made a day of twenty-four hours, which was divided into day and night (light and darkness) on יום 4. From יום 4 on, there was not a day of twenty-four hours, which was divided into day and night. It is self-evident in the Bible that the division of light from darkness and day from night mentioned in Genesis 1:4-5 is different from that mentioned in Genesis 1:14-19 executed on יום 4. It is from a purely human thinking to say that the earth rotates on its axis and revolves around the sun from the beginning before the solar system was created, since the Bible says, "And the evening and the morning were the first day." Genesis 1:14 clearly says that the solar system was initially made and four seasons appeared on 4 יום, in which the earth started rotating on its axis and revolving around the sun. So "the evening and the morning were the first day" does not mean that the first day and the night came from the earth's rotating on its axis and revolving around the sun. There was not the sun at that time and, accordingly, the earth could not yet rotate on its axis and revolve around the sun. Likewise, the evening and the morning did not appear due to the earth's rotating on its axis and revolving around the sun. "The evening and the morning were the first day" does not state that the day and the night came from the earth's rotating on its axis, but it just describes the first conditions of the primeval earth at the time of its creation.

Now, let me more closely analyze the statement in Genesis 1:14 so as to better understand סויה. "And God said, Let there be lights in the firmament of the heaven to divide the day from the night; and let them be for signs, and for seasons, and for days, and years." A day was first made by God on סויה 4.

סויה 1 (Gen. 1:5) in which there was spiritual light cannot mean a day of twenty-four hours since luminous bodies (stated in Gen. 1:14) were first invented on סויה 4. The seasons, days, and years were initially made on סויה 4. סויה 1 first appears in Genesis 1:5 before the system of a day of twenty-four hours came into being. So, it is supposed that סויה was initially used as a period or term. Another important thing to note here is that Genesis 1:14 records, "Let them be for signs, and for seasons, and for days, and years." It means seasons, days, and years came into being from סויה 4. In the Bible, the lights (the sun and the moon, etc.) have their own roles.

Some scientists assert that the primitive earth began rotating on its axis and revolving around the sun from the beginning. This contention is not in full accordance with the Bible, which clearly says in Genesis 1:14-19 that the sun, the moon, and stars were first made and the solar system was created on סויה 4. It is very clear that God's first order to give light (ריאהל in Hebrew) on the earth was made in Genesis 1:15 and 17. In other words, no light was given to the earth before the sun was made. On סויה 4, there came into being the rotation of the cycle, four seasons, and a day of twenty-four hours. So, from סויה

4, the calendar, the seasons, years, and days could be calculated. Before יום 4, there were no days or years nor the concept of four seasons. Nor could the number of days and years be calculated. Therefore, according to the narratives of Genesis 1, God did not create all creatures including the heaven and the earth and the universe about six thousand years ago (after the depravity of Adam) but an enormous number of years ago. The Biblical narratives are not agreeable to the contentions of modern theologies like dispensationalism and chroniclism and to theistic evolutionisms like the gap theory and the concordistic theory.

What is important is that before יום 4, there was not a day nor the conception or function (or use) of a day. In Genesis 1:16, the sun and the moon had their own roles: the greater light should rule the day and the lesser light rule the night. On the first day or יום 4, there initially came into being numerous stars like fixed stars, planets, and satellites including the solar system. Inventing a six day creation theory is not biblical but influenced by human preconceptions or traditions. It should be avoided.

Light appearing on יום 1 is not a visible ray of light but a spiritual light (1 Cor. 4:6, etc.) like a light of life (John 1:9). יום 1 does not mean a day of twenty-four hours but a period or term attested in Genesis 2:4, Job 14:5, 1 Samuel 2:19, and so forth. From יום 5, יום means a day of twenty-four hours. Of course, like יום 4, יום 5 or 6 may also mean a period or term. Before יום 4, there was not a day of twenty-four hours. According to Genesis 1:14-19, God created all creatures not in six days of 144 hours but in six יוםs.

Lastly, according to Genesis 1:27, a man and a woman were created on יום 6 out of nothing in God's image, after His likeness. However, according to Genesis 2:7 and 2:22, Adam was formed on a different day from that on which Eve was made. Furthermore, it is not that they were made out of nothing, but Adam was formed of the dust of the ground and Eve of a rib of Adam. It implies that the narrative of the creation of a man and a woman in chapter 1 is different from that in chapter 2.

There are numerous theological theories about the creation, such as gap theory, theme theory, subordinationism, reparation theory, dispensationalism, chronicle theory, literalism, abiogenesis, and filoque theory. However, it is self-evident from the descriptions in the Bible, especially Genesis 1, that the universe including man was not created in six days of 144 hours. It indicates that some of traditional Christian doctrines are derailed from the Bible. We must not follow human traditions but the original texts of the Bible.

Not all the human interpretations of the Bible are orthodox; some of them should be reinterpreted or rearranged. All Christian doctrines need be based on God's word, which must not be interpreted with any preconceptions or assumptions. Obedience is doing what the Bible says to do and not doing what it does not. Rejecting God's will (the Bible) and instead doing our own will is ideologically oppressing Jesus Christ and results in a stuffed specimen of God's laws. The Bible says, "Howbeit in vain do they worship me, teaching for doctrines the commandments of men" (Mark 7:7). Jesus also says, "Making the word of God of none effect through your tradition, which ye have delivered: and many such like things do ye" (Mark 7:13), and "And when he had called all the people unto him, he said unto them, Hearken unto me every one of you, and understand" (Mark 7:14). And God says, "This is my beloved Son, in whom I am well pleased; hear ye him" (Matt. 17:5).

Unlike in Genesis 1:27, in Genesis 2:7, God formed Adam of the dust of the ground and breathed into his nostrils the breath of life. God breathed the breath of life into the nostrils of Adam only. Consider Malachi 2:15, "And did not he make one? Yet had he the residue of the spirit. And wherefore one? That he might seek a godly seed. Therefore take heed to your spirit, and let none deal treacherously against the wife of his youth." Genesis 1:26 describes God's formation of man and woman in the image and likeness of God, but it does not mention that He breathed the spirit into their nostrils. However, Genesis 2:7 reports that the LORD God breathed the breath of life into the nostrils of Adam only (also see Mal. 2:15). Consider Genesis 2:7: "And the LORD God formed man of the dust of the ground, and breathed into his nostrils the breath of life; and man became a living soul." What is the breath of life? According to the original language, the word *breath* is used in Job 32:8 and 26:4 and Proverbs 20:27 and translated as "the spirit." And the life is in plural form and means the spirit plus the soul, which all humans have. It is why God the Creator is called the Father of spirits (Heb. 12:9).

Isaiah 57:16 says, "For I will not contend for ever, neither will I be always wroth: for the spirit should fail before me, and the souls which I have made." Zechariah 12:1 says, "The burden of the word of the LORD for Israel, saith the LORD, which stretcheth forth the heavens, and layeth the foundation of the earth, and formeth the spirit of man within him." Job 12:10 says, "In whose hand is the soul of every living thing, and the breath of all mankind." Job 32:8 says, "But there is a spirit in man: and the inspiration of the Almighty giveth them understanding." These verses clearly demonstrate that men are different from animals because they are spiritual beings. Proverbs 20:27 records, "The spirit of man is the candle of the LORD, searching all the inward parts of the belly." The Apostle Paul writes, "I pray God your whole spirit and soul and body be preserved blameless unto the coming of our Lord Jesus Christ" (1 Thess. 5:23). Hebrews 4:12, 1 Corinthians 2:11, 1 Corinthians 14:14-15 and many other verses say that human beings have a spirit. Also, consider "Then shall the dust [the body] return to the earth as it was: and the spirit shall return unto God who gave it" (Eccl. 12:7). When He died on the cross, Jesus cried, "Father, into thy hands I commend my spirit [רוח in Hebrew]" (Luke 23:46). As for Stephen, "And they stoned Stephen, calling upon God, and saying, Lord Jesus, receive my spirit" (Acts 7:59).

Consider Genesis 2:7, "And the LORD God formed man of the dust of the ground, and breathed into his nostrils the breath of life; and man became a living soul." And Genesis 2:8, "And the LORD God planted a garden eastward in Eden; and there he put the man whom he had formed." The man mentioned in Genesis 2:8 was made of the dust of the ground." Genesis 2:15 says, "And the LORD God took the man, and put him into the garden of Eden to dress it and to keep it." We don't know how long the man had dressed and kept the garden, but it is clear that he did not give the fauna of animals their names in a day of twenty-four hours.

Carl von Linne (1707-1778), a Swedish biologist, authored a famous book entitled *The System of Nature*, in which he groups creatures into kingdoms, divisions, classes, orders, families, genuses, and species. He did not give creatures their names but just classified them; and it took him scores of years. Some time after the creation (Gen. 2:18,20), "the LORD God said It is not good that the man should be alone; I will make him an help meet for him" (Gen. 2:18). And the LORD God caused a deep sleep to fall upon Adam and he slept: and he took one of his ribs, and closed up the flesh instead thereof. God did not create Eve out of nothing but made her with a rib of her husband. And Eve was called woman by Adam (Gen. 2:23). Man (רבג in Hebrew is different from male in English; see Gen. 1:27) first mentioned in Genesis 2:24 refers to שׁיא, from which השׁיאא (woman) is derived.

God made Eve since "It is not good that the man should be alone" (Gen. 2:18). It implies that Adam and Eve were not made on the same day. Genesis 2:20 records, "for Adam there was not found an help meet for him." It implies that Adam was trying to find an help meet among creatures made during the six days stated in Genesis 1. It suggests that Adam and Eve were not created during the six days. The Bible clearly says in chapter 1 that a man and a woman were created on the same day through God's word. In chapter 2, Adam and Eve were made separately with a material. Isaiah 43:7 contains the verbs used in chapters 1 and 2 of Genesis to describe the formation of man. Isaiah 43:7 says, "I have created him [sons and daughters mentioned in Isa. 43:6] for my glory, I have formed him; yea, I have made him." Here, the man means Adam who is Eve's husband and a help meet means a counter partner or a companion. Therefore, it implies that a woman is intended for her husband, the role of a woman is to help and support her husband, and there is equal relationship between and the man and the woman. However, after they ate the fruit of the tree of knowledge, their relationship changed so that he shall rule over her (Gen. 3:16, 1 Cor. 11:3).

God did directly order not Eve but Adam not to eat the fruit of the tree of knowledge (Gen. 2:16-17). Adam by himself did not pick up and eat the fruit of the tree of knowledge, but he is guilty of not ruling over Eve properly. Their actions are not the same but their sins are equal. It is never true that God made Adam and Eve on the same day. This is theologically very important. According to Genesis 1:27, God created a man and a woman out of nothing on the same day or the 6th day of creation. In contrast, according to Genesis 2:7 and 2:22, Adam and Eve were made with a material on a separate day. And unlike Genesis 1, in Genesis 2:7 God breathed the breath of life into the nostrils of Adam. Neither is it true that they were allowed to be fruitful, multiply and fill on the earth but to live only in the garden of Eden, where protection was provided to them (Gen. 2:8).

The creation story in chapters 1 and 2 of Genesis is also explained in Isaiah 43:7. "Even every one that is called by my name: for I have created him for my glory, I have formed him; yea, I have made him." When Cain, who is the first son of Adam, killed his brother and was an exile, he cried to God, "it shall come to pass, that every one that findeth me shall slay me" (Gen. 4:14). This implies that there were at that time many people on the earth besides the family of Adam. Then "Cain went out from the presence of the LORD, and dwelt in the land of Nod, on the east of Eden. And Cain knew his wife; and she conceived, and bare Enoch" (Gen. 4:16,17). This implies that Cain married a woman of the offspring of those who had been fruitful, multiplied and filled the earth.

Usually, people explain that the man and woman in Genesis 1 are the same as those described more in detail in Genesis 2. This explanation is a human imagination and fiction, like a contention that Lucifer is Satan (Isa. 14:12-15; Eze. 28:12-19) and that the morning star is Jesus (Rev. 2:38, 22:16). Lucifer means a luminous body or illuminating star and is translated as a morning star in English and a day star in the Korean edition. According to Revelation 22:16, Jesus is the root and the offspring of David, and the bright and morning star, which is not Satan. No verse in the Bible says that Lucifer is Satan. According to the Bible, Stan is called dragon, old serpent or devil in Revelation 2:9, 20:2, Job 1:6, 2:1, Zechariah 3:2, Judas 1:9, and Matthew 4:1.

Satan is also called Beelzebub (Mark 12:24, 27; Mark 3:22, etc.). Some scholars divided researches on Stan into satanology and demonology. The word Beelzebub is derived from Baal (1 Kings 18:19-29; 2 Kings 1:2-3, 6, 16), which means a god of bottle-green flies, scornfully called by Jews, or the master of the house (Matt. 10:25). Satan is also called Belial (Deut. 13:13; Judg. 19:22; 1 Kings 21:10; 2 Cor. 6:15;), which is not an official designation of Satan. Some wrongfully think that Abaddon or Apollyon, the king over the locusts in Revelation 9:11, also refers to Satan. Some think that Abaddon, which is the angel of the bottomless pit, is Uriel attested in 1 Enoch 20:2, but it is not, since it is an angel of God and cannot be the ruler of locusts. Still some contend that leviathan (Isa. 27:1; Job 3:8, 41:1; Ps. 74:14, etc.) is another designation of Satan. In Isaiah 27:1, leviathan is described as the piercing serpent, that crooked serpent, or the dragon that is in the sea. These three are correspondent to the three unclean spirits: the trinity of Satan comprising the dragon, the beast, and the false prophet stated in Revelation 16:13. The trinity of Satan seems to be a generic term for evil on the earth. Leviathan is not an official designation of Satan. For your information, the following are the designations of an evil spirit: demon, goblin, bogy or bogeyman, specter, monster, apparition, phantom, ghost, fairy, elf, and dotage. Christians should not and must not deny or reproach God's written word.

Consider the following verses: "For it is impossible for those who were once enlightened, and have tasted of the heavenly gift, and were made partakers of the Holy Ghost, and have tasted the good word of God, and the powers of the world to come, If they shall fall away, to renew them again unto repentance; seeing they crucify to themselves the Son of God afresh, and put him to an open shame" (Heb. 6:4-6). "For if we sin wilfully after that we have received the knowledge of the truth, there remaineth no more sacrifice for sins, But a certain fearful looking for of judgment and fiery indignation, which shall devour the adversaries" (Heb. 10:26,27). "Making the word of God of none effect through your tradition, which ye have delivered: and many such like things do ye" (Mark 7:13). "And these things, brethren, I have in a figure transferred to myself and to Apollos for your sakes; that ye might learn in us not to think of men above that which is written, that no one of you be puffed up for one against another" (1 Cor. 4:6). "Add thou not unto his words, lest he reprove thee, and thou be found a liar" (Prov. 30:6). "For I testify unto every man that heareth the words of the prophecy of this book, If any man shall add unto these things, God shall add unto him the plagues that are written in this book. And if any man shall take away from the words of the book of this prophecy, God shall take away his part out of the book of life, and out of the holy city, and from the things which are written in this book" (Rev. 22:18-19).

Now, in the following, let me sum up what we have considered concerning the doctrine of man and what composes a man.

Dichotomy and Trichotomy

Dichotomy contends that a human is composed of two parts: body and soul. In dichotomy, soul comprises soul and spirit. When a human dies, soul is separated from body, which will perish away. Plato (427-347 BC) contends that the body is correspondent to the shell of oyster and the soul to the flesh of oyster; body will perish away but soul, which is not created, will not.

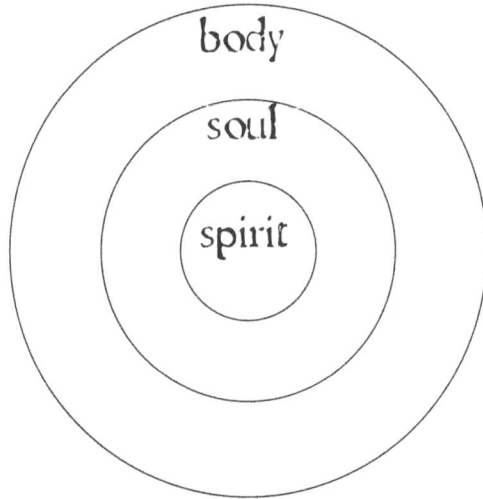

Trichotomy contends that a human being is composed of spirit, soul, and body (Isa. 57:16; Zech. 12:1; Job 12:10, 32:8; Prov. 20:27; 1 Thess. 5:23; Heb. 4:12; 1 Cor. 2:11, 14:14-15), each of which has its own role and function. All animals including microorganisms like bacteria have body and soul; however, only men have spirit. The spirit is surrounded by the soul, which is surrounded by the body. The body is controlled by the soul, which is controlled by the spirit controlled by the Creator.

Now I would like to look in more detail at the body, the soul and the spirit.

(1) Body

All living things including human beings and microorganisms in the world have a form—the body. According to the original language of the Bible, the physical body (σῶμα) (1 Thess. 5:23) also means flesh (σάρξ) (1 John 2:16), which is a sinful nature of men. The flesh controls the body described in the trichotomy. The body of a human being when it dies will return to the dust, out of which it is taken (Gen. 3:19; Eccl. 12:7) and so will all creatures. The body is a matter; it grows old or diseased over time and is limited in time and space. It cannot be reproduced after it dies. In the Bible, the body of a human being is called a tabernacle, but the resurrection body is called a house (2 Cor. 5:1). Only the bodies of human beings will be resurrected for judgment since only they have a spirit. The resurrection body is a special body different from our normal one since it does not grow old or diseased but transcends the boundaries of time and space.

(2) Soul

All creatures including human beings have the soul (Job 12:10). The soul is the life of all creatures (1 Thess. 2:8; Rev. 2:10). The soul is the main agent for creatures to think, feel, and sense. It also represents an ego (Luke 1:46). When they die, the soul of creatures also stops functioning. When the soul has left, the heartbeat stops and breathing and brain activities cease, which results in death.

(3) Spirit

The spirit is possessed only by man, who is the lord of all creation. It is not materialistic or made of something. It is specially given by God to humans (Gen. 2:7). "And did not he make one? Yet had he the residue of the spirit. And wherefore one? That he might seek a godly seed" (Mal. 2:15). God the Father of spirits (Heb. 12:9) gives human beings their spirit when they are born so that they may be a spiritual being (Isa. 57:16; 1 Thess. 5:23).

There are several theories about the provision of the spirit. One contends that the spirit is created and given by God to human beings when they are born (or conceived). Another believes that the spirit is previously prepared and exists ages prior to the birth of a human and is given to each person when he or she is born. Still another asserts that God the Father of spirits (Heb. 12:9) breathes into only Adam His spirit (Gen. 2:7; Mal. 2:15), which is partaken by his offspring. Therefore, the spirit can commune with God (1 Cor. 2:11; Rom. 8:16). The spirit also transcends the boundaries of time and space (1 Cor. 5:3) and it is immortal and immaterial since, like the angels, it cannot die anymore (Luke 20:36). When men die, their body and soul pass away but their spirit, being permanently existing, comes out of their body and goes to the paradise (παράδεισος in Greek) or Hades (Luke 16:22-23, 23:43; 1 Pet. 3:19; Rev. 20:13), (Eccl. 12:7; Matt. 22:30; Rev. 21:4; Luke 20:36). That is why dead men are described as sleeping (John 11:11; 1 Thess. 4:13, etc.) and it is said in the Bible that the graves were opened and many bodies of the saints that slept arose (Matt. 27:52).

Some think that Purgatory (1 Pet. 3:19-20, 4:6) is represented by Sheol (שאול in Hebrew) in the Old Testament or Hades (άδης in Greek) in the New Testament. Sheol (Gen. 37:35, etc.) is translated as Hades or a tomb to depict the state of death. Hades (Luke 16:23, etc.) is said to be a place of punishment in contrast to the paradise (Luke 23:43). Hades is not hell, a place of everlasting punishment, and different from the "dark underground pit" (ταρταρωθας in Greek) mentioned only once in the Bible, in 2 Peter 2:4, a place where depraved spirits are kept till the final judgment.

Eleven Places for Human Beings After Death

According to the Bible, there are eleven places that human beings can go after death in the so-called world of spirits, which is an intermediate state between death and resurrection. They are paradise (Luke 23:43), Hades (Luke 16:23), grave (Gen. 37:35), prison (1 Pet. 3:19-20, etc.), Purgatory (1 Pet. 4:6), dark underground pit (2 Pet. 2:4), the bottomless pit (Rev. 9:1), heaven (Matt. 4:17), hell (Matt. 5:22), the lake of fire (Rev. 20:14), and a lake of fire burning with brimstone (Rev. 19:20).

(1) Paradise (παράδεισος in Greek and גן עדן in Hebrew, Luke 23:43)

According to the Septuagint, paradise is identified with the Garden of Eden. Paradise is mentioned only three time in the Old Testament: Nehemiah 2:8, Ecclesiastes 2:5, and Song of Solomon 4:13. In Genesis 13:10, it is also mentioned as the garden of the Lord. In the Old Testament times, Jews thought that paradise was a place where righteous souls reside after their death but before resurrection, such as heaven or the Garden of Eden stated in Chapters 2 and 3 of Genesis 2 and 3. Paradise is also attested three times in the New Testament: Luke's Gospel 23:43, 2 Corinthians 12:4, and Revelation 2:7. Abraham's bosom (Luke 16:23) may be also considered as paradise in contrast to Hades, but it is not certain. Paradise is clearly stated in Luke 23:43, where Jesus says to the malefactor crucified on His right (named Dismas according apocryphal Acts of Pilate), "Verily I say unto thee, Today shalt thou be with me in paradise." In 2 Corinthians 12:1-3, Paul writes about his experience of being caught up to the third heaven, which is identified with paradise.

Revelation 2:7 mentions "the tree of life, which is in the midst of the paradise of God." In the New Testament, paradise is limited to a temporary dwelling where righteous souls stay between death and resurrection and where righteous spirits are waiting for their resurrection of life and looking forward to entering heaven after the final judgment before God's white throne (John 5:29). In sheer contrast, evil sinners are agonizing in Hades and waiting to be punished in hell after the final judgment and resurrection of damnation (John 5:29). After death, the human body is buried in the earth and the spirit will leave the body and not die or perish (1 Cor. 15:53; Luke 20:36) but go to paradise or Hades and wait for resurrection. Paradise is a temporary abode where good spirits stay after death and wait for entering heaven (Luke 23:43). Jesus says that human beings will go after death to a temporary abode of paradise (Luke 23:43) or Hades (Luke 16:23) i.e., hell (Mark 9:43).

(2) Hades (ᾅδης in Greek, mentioned eleven times in Matt. 11:23, 16:18; Luke 10:15, 16:23; Acts 2:27, 31; Rom. 10:7; Rev. 1:18, 6:8, 20:13-14)

Hades stands in contrast to paradise. Hades is a place where evil sinners abide temporarily after death waiting for resurrection and judgment.

Jesus describes paradise and Hades in Luke's Gospel 16:19-31. In the Old Testament, Hades is expressed as Sheol, which is considered not just as a place of torture. According to the Old Testament, both good and evil sinners go down to Sheol (Gen. 37:35). According to the New Testament, Hades is a place of torture, where evil sinners stay temporarily after death and before resurrection, waiting for the judgment before the white throne (Luke 16:23). Hades is different from hell (γέενα in Greek), which is spiritual beings' abode in everlasting torture and to which they go after resurrection and judgment. When they are clothed with their resurrection body or spiritual body after resurrection (1 Cor. 15:44), the spirits can around move in hell or heaven as they wish. However, before they are resurrected, the spirits can see, sense, and communicate with others but cannot move as they want because they do not yet have their resurrection body (Luke 16:23-24), like a pupa before turning to a moth. In this world, a human being has a form, in which the spirit is. But after death, the form is contained in the spirit.

The resurrection body, with bones and flesh, or a spiritual body (Luke 24:39), can be touched by the hands of a natural man (1 Cor. 15:44). The spirits in Hades are a state like a criminal in a detention center waiting for trial (the judgment before the white throne) before being convicted and put to the prison (hell). The spirits being tortured in Hades, where they are regretting their wrongdoing (Luke 16:28), cannot be saved, just put to judgment after resurrection (John 5:29). Therefore, we must believe in Jesus and be saved in this present world. Some assert that one can be saved when he repents even in Hades, by citing this verse, "For for this cause was the gospel preached also to them that are dead, that they might be judged according to men in the flesh, but live according to God in the spirit" (1 Pet. 4:6). However, according to 1 Peter 3:19,20, the spirits in prison are none other than those disobedient in the days of Noah.

To sum up, Hades is a temporary abode of torture to which evil sinners go after death, and it is different from hell and in contrast to paradise.

(3) Grave (Sheol or שאול in Hebrew, mentioned sixty-six times in the Old Testament, including Gen. 37:35 and Job 7:9)
Sheol is expressed as a grave thirty-five times, Hades twenty-seven times and a pit three times in the Old Testament. It is the next world, to which both good sinners and evil sinners go after death and in which they can meet their forefathers (Gen. 37:35, 49:33; Job 14:13; 2 Sam. 12:23). According to the Septuagint, Sheol is expressed as Hades. It is understood as a place for burying a dead body.

(4) Prison (φυλακή in Greek, 1 Pet. 3:18-20, 1 Pet. 4:6)
"By which also he went and preached unto the spirits in prison; which sometime were disobedient, when once the longsuffering

of God waited in the days of Noah, while the ark was a preparing, wherein few, that is, eight souls were saved by water" (1 Pet. 3:19-20). "For for this cause was the gospel preached also to them that are dead, that they might be judged according to men in the flesh, but live according to God in the spirit" (1 Pet. 4:6).

This prison is very controversial along with the Purgatory taught in Catholicism. Controversies around 1 Peter 3:18-20 and 4:1 were severe during the Reformation, and they have been aggravated since then. Anyhow, the prison stated in 1 Peter 3:19 should be interpreted as being different from Sheol or Hades. The spirits in prison are not the people unreached with the gospel but the people living at the time of Noah (1 Pet. 3:20) when the earth was corrupt before God and filled with violence. At the time of Noah, people would not return to God but disobeyed and were corrupt (Gen. 6:11). They ridiculed the word of God to punish this world (Gen. 6:13) and made sport of Noah, who was building a wooden ark. After being crucified, Jesus Christ in His spirit went down to them and preached the gospel for their salvation (1 Pet. 3:20).

Some say 1 Peter 3:20 is hard to interpret since it seems to demonstrate that men may have an opportunity to accept the gospel and be everlastingly saved even after death when they receive the Savior. The problem is that there are few Bible verses that give a decisive answer to this issue. The Bible should not be excessively paraphrased but interpreted strictly and conservatively. In other words, the prison should be interpreted and understood only after considering 1 Peter 3:18-20 and 1 Peter 4:6 carefully. Being different from Hades, the prison is a place where only those having disobeyed the word of God at the time of Noah are shut up (1 Pet. 4:6). To them, an opportunity was given to be saved after death when Jesus preached the gospel in prison (1 Pet. 3:20, 4:6). Here, we must recall Matthew 20:1-16, where Jesus teaches about laborers in the vineyard. Only one denarius is given as daily wages to each of the vineyard laborers, of whom some worked from early in the morning (figuratively, the time between Adam and Noah), some from the third hour (between Noah and Moses), some from the sixth hour (between Moses and Jesus) and some from the ninth hour (between Jesus Christ and the end of the world).

This teaching shows that the same wages shall be given to the saints in the Old Testament age (Jews) and the New Testament age (Gentiles) according to the decision or grace and favor of the owner of the vineyard, or the will of the Creator Jehovah God. Concerning how to obtain salvation, the same applies to the people living in the Old Testament age and those in the New Testament age, including unreached people with the gospel. There is no discrimination against them all. Salvation shall be given to them not because they believe in Jesus and accept the gospel but they have no sin. Anyone who has no sin can be saved and go to heaven, whether they live in the Old Testament age or in the New Testament age. Jesus came into this world in order to remove sins from human beings. If human beings had not had any sin, it would not be necessary that Jesus should come into this world and for people to believe in Jesus. The only way for people to get their sins forgiven is to believe in Jesus, who was crucified on behalf of them to remit their sins. Anyone without sin can go to heaven. Such people shall not be saved as have not heard the gospel or have heard but rejected it, whether they live in the Old Testament age or in the New Testament age.

A scheme of such a kind seems to be unfair and unreasonable to those living in the Old Testament age or the unreached people in the New Testament age, but the decision is made by the potter, who makes a vessel in his hand as seemed good to him (Jer. 18:4). Therefore, people living in this present age shall give thanks to God for His grace and favor. In the future, people shall be blessed to live in the millennial kingdom after the second coming of Jesus. If human beings can be given another opportunity to be saved after death, why is it that Jesus says, "Wherefore if thy hand or thy foot offend thee, cut them off, and cast them from thee: it is better for thee to enter into life halt or maimed, rather than having two hands or two feet to be cast into everlasting fire. And if thine eye offend thee, pluck it out, and cast it from thee: it is better for thee to enter into life with one eye, rather than having two eyes to be cast into hell fire" (Matt. 18:8-9)? No other Bible verses than 1 Peter 3:19 and 4:6 suggest that another opportunity will be given to be saved after death. The Bible clearly teaches that there shall be no opportunity to be forgiven of sins after death (Matt. 5:22-24, 16:26; Mark 9:43-45; Luke 12:20; Heb. 6:6).

(5) Purgatory (1 Pet. 4:6, 3:19)
"For for this cause was the gospel preached also to them that are dead, that they might be judged according to men in the flesh, but live according to God in the spirit"

(1 Pet. 4:6). "By which also he went and preached unto the spirits in prison; which sometime were disobedient, when once the longsuffering of God waited in the days of Noah, while the ark was a preparing, wherein few, that is, eight souls were saved by water" (1 Pet. 3:19-20).

Based on these verses, Catholicism teaches the doctrine of Purgatory, which is different from Hades and is a territory between heaven and hell, where imperfect believers stay and are disciplined for refinement after death. That is why Catholicism recognizes the efficacy of good deeds for salvation or the

salvation through good works. Masses and prayers are presented for the indulgences of the spirits abiding in Purgatory so that
their sins may be lessened or forgiven. First Corinthians 3:15
and other verses are cited to maintain that imperfect believers
or spirits go to heaven after being made perfect through disciplines in Purgatory. For the doctrine of Purgatory, Catholicism
cites such verses as Isaiah 4:4; Micah 7:8; Ezra 9:11; Malachi
3:2-3; Matthew 12:32, 16:19; John 20:23; 1 Corinthians 3:13-15,
15:29, and 1 Peter 3:19, 4:6.

Catholicism teaches that Purgatory is different from Sheol
or Hades and that prison mentioned in 1 Peter 3:19 is Purgatory.
If "the spirits in prison" include those who died in the New
Testament age, the doctrine of purgatory is right. However, the
Bible clearly says that the spirits in prison are those living in the
days of Noah (1 Pet. 3:20). If the doctrine of Purgatory is right,
Jesus must still remain and spread the gospel in Purgatory and
the spirits refined through disciplines in Purgatory must still
continue moving from there to paradise. On the contrary,
the Bible says that after crucifixion Jesus went down to prison
and preached the gospel there and then resurrected in three
days through God's works. After that, He spoke of the things
pertaining to the kingdom of God for forty days on the earth
(Acts 1:3) and then ascended to heaven (Acts 1:9). Therefore,
it needs to be confirmed that the spirits in prison mentioned in
1 Peter 3:19 are those living in the Noah age when he built the
ark. It seems that the purgatorial theory was generated when
the verse of 1 Peter 3:19 was broadly interpreted and the other
verses are considered meaningless, except for 1 Corinthians
15:29, which is considered hard to understand and in which
Apostle Paul stresses the resurrection of dead bodies.

First Corinthians 15:29 and 30 record, "Else what shall they
do which are baptized for the dead, if the dead rise not at all?

why are they then baptized for the dead? And why stand we in jeopardy every hour? And why stand we in jeopardy every hour?" According to the original text, the word 'for' (υπέρ in Greek) in these verses may have three meanings: "up," "in place of," or "concerning" (John 1:30). If the word has the meaning of "concerning," then verse 29 may be translated as, "If the resurrection of the dead is not true, what is the use of the baptism of those baptized before death?" And verse 30 means that we stand in jeopardy every hour because we will have resurrection after death.

Prelate Chrysostom has a story. When some Marchionists, disciples of Marchion, sat under the bed of the dead and the baptizer asked the dead if he would be willing to be baptized, the one under the bed responded that he would be baptized on behalf of the dead. And vicarious baptism was executed. The above-said Bible verses show that such a baptism was still practiced in the days of Apostle Paul among Corinthian church members. About a vicarious baptism for the dead, Paul says nothing negative or positive. The main point Paul wants to elucidate in 1 Corinthians 15 is not a vicarious baptism for the dead but the resurrection of believers after death.

Conclusively, there is no decisive Bible verse that supports the doctrine of Purgatory.

(6) Dark Underground Pit (ταρταρωθας in Greek, 2 Pet. 2:4)
In the Orthodox Bible, the dark underground pit is used only once, in 2 Peter 2:4. In the Apocrypha, it is used in Enoch 10:14 and 12:13 to denote a place where the angels degenerating into the bottom of Hades are locked until the judgment before the white throne. Some people contend that this pit is a place where the angels who kept not their first estate but left their own habitation, according to Judas 1:6, are temporarily

shut till the judgment before the white throne. The pit is different from Hades, which is a place for evil sinners to enter after death, or from hell, which is a place of the final everlasting punishment, since the pit is a temporary abode of punishment for degenerate angels. Like Sheol or Hades, the pit is a place where evil sinners are temporarily shut in before going to their everlasting punishment or a lake of fire burning with brimstone (Rev. 19:20, 20:10). Some scholars understand that the pit is the deepest part of hell. The dark underground pit or chains of darkness is different from a lake of fire burning with brimstone (Rev. 19:20, 20:10), which is an abode of the final everlasting punishment for Satan and his angels (the beast, false prophet and evil spirit; Rev. 20:10).

Human beings after death got to paradise or Hades, their temporary abode before entering heaven or hell, the final everlasting abode. Likewise evil sinners go into the dark underground pit before entering a lake of fire burning with brimstone, which is an abode of their everlasting punishment. Since spirits cannot die (Luke 20:36), they stay in the pit before going to their everlasting punishment and torture. And the spirits sent forth to minister for those who will be heirs of salvation (Heb. 1:14) cannot die after being created but stay permanently in heaven to minister for God's foster children (Rom. 8:15).

(7) *Bottomless pit* (αβυσσας in Greek and תהום in Hebrew, used thirty-seven times, in Rev. 9:1, 2, 11, 11:7, 17:8, 20:1; 30 times in Gen. 1:2; Ps. 71:20)

The bottomless pit is translated as the deep in Genesis 1:2, which means a boiling bottomless abyss. This abyss is different from hell or Hades and is a place where Satan will be locked in during the millennium.

Therefore, it is different from a lake of fire burning with brimstone, which is Satan's abode for everlasting punishment. According to the Apocrypha, including 1 Enoch 18:12-16, 19:1-2, 21:1-6 and others, the bottomless pit is a waterless, burning, fearful, and chaotic place that is endlessly deep. We usually imagine that the pit is like a big pot or jar with limitless depth. Satan will be shut in the bottomless pit during the millennium and then be loosed for a season so that he may deceive the nations. After that, he will be taken once again and cast into the lake of fire and brimstone, where the beast and the false prophet are, and will be tormented day and night for ever and ever (Rev. 20:3, 10). Abaddon (אבדן) in Hebrew or Apollyon (απολλυων) in Greek is the king of the bottomless pit. Abaddon is different from the angel who has the key to the bottomless pit and a great chain in his hand (Rev. 20:1). According to 1 Enoch 19:1 and 20:2, this angel is Uriel, one of seven archangels. (The others are: Raphael, Raquel, Michael, Sariel, Gabriel, and Ramiel). Some think that the angel is Michael, who contended with the devil who disputed about the body of Moses (Judas 1:9).

(8) *Heaven* (ή βασιλεία των ουραν in Greek, the kingdom of heaven, or new heaven and new earth; used about thirty times in the Bible, including Matt. 4:17, 5:3; Rev. 21:1)
Heaven is also expressed as "the kingdom of heaven" or "the kingdom of God." Jews are unwilling to use the word God; so they coined the expression "the kingdom of heaven," which is used in Matthew's Gospel. Elsewhere, the gospels use "the kingdom of God."

Heaven is different from paradise, which is a temporary abode after death, and different from the millennium (Rev. 20:2-6). Heaven is an everlasting abode of believers and an everlasting country of Christians. Heaven is different from the kingdom of Messiah in the Old Testament, which some Jews consider as a future kingdom of God. There is no devil or evil in heaven, where glory is given only to God in truth. In heaven, people permanently enjoy a joyful life in a world, where there is no aging, disease, torture, and pain but happiness and peace. Why is there no night in heaven (Rev. 21:23)? Because darkness (night) is a result of evil, and there is no Satan or evil in heaven. In heaven, God and Jesus Christ always shed God's love (1 John 4:8, 16), truth (Ps. 119:142; John 17:17) and light (1 John 1:5; John 8:12), like the sun and the moon (Rev. 21:23).

Initial apostles accepted, reinforced and spread Jesus Christ's teachings about heaven. In particular, the epistles of Peter and Paul and the Revelation of John are a revelation of hopes for the kingdom of heaven. The gospel focuses on heaven and hell, which are places spirits will go to after death. Like almost all the other religions, Christianity converges its teachings on future heaven. Christianity without heaven is like an egg without the yolk. In modern times, people's view of the next world faded so much that they will not accept the Bible as God's word. They regard it as just a myth and rely more on human assertions or thoughts. As a result, Christianity is considered simply as a religion of morals and culture, or as a means for political or social reform and liberation. Moreover, modern Christians do not lead a life of faith with a purely religious motive but with a view to rising in this world. Christians' everlasting home country is in the next world, to which they look forward to going in hope.

(9) *Hell* (γέεννα in Greek and םוניה in Hebrew, Josh. 18:16; Matt. 5:22, 29, 30, 10:28, 18:9, 23:15, 33; Mark 9:43, 45, 47; Luke 12:5; Jam. 3:6; used twelve times in the New Testament)

In the Old Testament, hell is translated as Hinnom in Hebrew and Gehenna in Greek. The valley of Hinnom (Josh. 18:16) was a valley south of Jerusalem, where Moloch (the god of Semites) was worshiped in older days (1 Kings 11:7; 2 Chr. 28:3, 33:6). In the valley, an iron image of the god was burned hot in order to represent hell and a child was burnt as an offering in the arms of the god. Hell is referred to as the lake of fire (Rev. 20:14-15), which is not a temporary abode of punishment for evil sinners but an everlasting abode of punishment for them. Hell is an everlasting abode of torture and punishment after the judgment before the white throne for evil sinners, who have pursued after selfish love. Jesus says of hell, "Where their worm dieth not, and the fire is not quenched" (Mark 9:48). In hell, every one will be salted with hot fire and every sacrifice will be continually salted and tortured with salt (Mark 9:49). In such hell fire, spirits with resurrection body will not be burned and die because they belong to a non-materialistic world, which is not composed of aging or consuming materials.

A resurrection body is a special invulnerable or immortal spiritual body (1 Cor. 15:44) that will not be bruised or damaged. Unlike a natural body, the spiritual body will not age, decay, or burn. The spiritual body also has flesh, bones, and senses (Luke 24:39), for it is a special changed body (1 Cor. 15:44). It is kept in hell and suffers everlasting torture, fire, and agony. That is why Jesus says, "And if thy hand offend thee, cut it off: it is better for thee to enter into life maimed, than having two hands to go into hell, into the fire that never shall be quenched ... where their worm dieth not, and the fire is not quenched" (Matt. 18:8-9; Mark 9:43, 46). In order not to enter such a permanently agonizing and torturing fire, we must believe in Jesus Christ and have the original sin and our actual sins forgiven through the redemption made by Jesus when He

was crucified. Anyone, rich or poor, knowledgeable or ignorant, noble or humble, can have their sins forgiven and go to
heaven if they believe in Jesus before they die.

Tomorrow is too late. No procrastination! None of us knows
when we will die. We must not put off believing in Jesus and receiving salvation to possess eternal life.

(10) Fire (Rev. 20:14-15)

Both Hades and death shall be plunged into the fire (Rev.
20:14). In the end, the first heaven and the first earth will pass
away (Rev. 21:1). Whoever was not found written in the book of
life will be cast into the lake of fire (Rev. 20:15), which is considered analogous to hell. However, this fire is different from
the lake of burning sulfur (Rev. 19:20), into which Satan and
his angels (the beast and the false prophet) will be cast (Rev.
20:10). No Bible verse says that wicked sinners along with Satan
will be cast into the lake of fire burning with brimstone.

To sum up, the lake of fire is an everlasting abode of punishment for evil sinners after God's final judgment before the
white throne. It is the same as hell, which is mentioned in
Matthew 5:22 and Mark 9:43, among others. Going into the
lake of fire signifies eternal severance from God. Therefore,
the fire must be a place of eternal punishment for evil sinners.

(11) Lake of burning sulfur or the lake of fire burning with brimstone (Rev. 19–21)

A lake of fire burning with brimstone is an abode of eternal
punishment for Satan, the beast, and the false prophet, as well
as Satan's angels, who are evil spirits. The lake of fire burning with brimstone is different from chains of darkness or the
bottomless pit. The lake is a place of the final permanent punishment and torture not for human beings but for the devil

and his angels. In the Bible, sulfur and fire are described as a means of God's punishment, which is attested in Genesis 19:24, reporting the punishment of Sodom and Gomorrah.

The lake of fire burning with brimstone is unlike hell, which evil sinners will finally enter, but may be called hell for Satan and his evil spirits. In the fire of sulfur, Satan will meet the beast and the false prophet, the three of which comprise the trinity of devil, since the abode is prepared for devil and his angels to be punished forever.

I would like to summarize the above-mentioned eleven places for men after death. When they die, the spirits of human beings go to paradise or Hades. At the end of this world, the spirits of all human beings will be resurrected from paradise or Hades and put to God's judgment before the white throne on the earth after the millennium. Then, according to the judgment, the spirits go to heaven or hell permanently. Satan and his angels or evil spirits will be put to permanent torture in a lake of fire burning with brimstone (Rev. 20:10). God's angels will minister saints or heirs of salvation in heaven (Heb. 1:14). Then, this world, heaven (the universe) and death will exist no more (Rev. 20:14, 21:1). But a lake of fire burning with brimstone, hell (fire) and heaven will stand permanently. Human beings with their spirits will live through the millennial kingdom at the end of the last days after the second coming of Jesus (Rev. 20:4-8).

When Jesus comes down to earth the second time, the souls of those who are beheaded for the witness of Jesus and for the word of God and who have not worshipped the beast, neither his image, neither have received his mark (which is a spiritual seal) upon their foreheads, or in their hands, will have part in the first resurrection, live and reign with Christ for a thousand years (Rev. 20:4-6). Unlike the seal (σφραγίδα), the mark

(χάραγμα) will be put not spiritually but physically on foreheads or in right hands.

The Mark of the Beast

The mark of the beast, or 666, is mentioned in Revelation
13. At the end of the last days, before the second coming of
Jesus, antichrists (1 John 2:18; 2 Thess. 2:3) will appear and,
leading the single government of the world, the second beast
(Rev. 13:16) will unify the political and religious circles so as to
force every one in the world to get his mark. This is the number 666 inscribed on an electronic chip (Rev. 13:16-18).

This number is shown on a bar code for all the commodities that are sold nowadays; there is a number 6 on the front
part, the middle part and the end part of a bar code. The
code, developed in the 1970s along with computers, has the
same function as integrated circuit cards like smart cards. The
electronic chip is called a veri-chip (*veri* is an abbreviation of
verification) when the number 666 is inscribed on a general
commodity, and it is also called a biochip, corresponding to
radio frequency identification, when the number is inscribed
on a human body. The chip was developed in 2003 by Applied
Digital Solution Company located in Florida and approved in
2004 by the U.S. Food and Drug Administration. In the future,
currency, checks, and credit cards will be replaced by an electronic chip with the beast's mark on it. Those having this mark
will be able to sell or buy something (Rev. 13:17). In the future,
all payments will be made with a biochip or veri-chip.

Also, the beast's mark will not only function as currency
but will store all personal information like social status and financial condition. For example, a biochip may contain information on a person's bank balance, medical history, employ-
ment history, and so forth. Therefore, those without the beast's

mark cannot sell or buy goods or enter government offices, airports, hospitals, and other public places if they do not carry the mark that serves as their identification. On February 2, 1997, the legislature of the U.S. state of Georgia passed a bill to put a biochip called a general identification system into a human body. The use of a biochip is being tested not only in the United States but also in Spain and other European countries. It is expected that the chip will be quickly spread around the world before long and, will one day be obligatorily for everybody (Rev. 13:17). The use of a veri-chip or a biochip will bring epoch-making changes to the inventory management and customer services. With this system, large quantities of commodities can be checked automatically without counting each item, so that shops may no longer need cashiers.

Prices of commodities can be paid automatically with a biochip (the beast's mark) on a human body. Moreover, without a wallet, you can purchase drinks or other necessities from a swimming pool or a public bathroom since you can conveniently make payment with the mark (a biochip) on your body. Under the single world government of the antichrist, it is easy to control secret information, prevent appropriation of personal identification, and head off terrorist attacks.

Why should society not take advantage of such a convenient and useful development as the biochip? You will understand the reason, when you fully know the functions of the chip. The human body, including hair and saliva, is composed of about sixty trillion cells, in each of whose nucleus there are about thirty-one trillion pairs of double helix structured gene or DNA (deoxyribonucleic acid), which contain all the information on the cell's function. DNA is often compared to a set of blueprints for the body. In about three million of the genes, human beings are different from animals, including a monkey.

There are 128 memory gene marks (DNA-codes) in the bio-chip. For example, a biochip can find damaged genes in a dementia patient and freshly renew them. Today, such a biochip is inserted into animals to manage and control them. In the future, when the biochip will be developed more and infused into the skin of a human being, a monitor that detects cell nuclei in the body will be able to understand even a human's thinking. Furthermore, manipulating the monitor can change or control one's thinking. Therefore, a man who has such a chip in his body will be a virtual cyborg.

A veri-chip has been developed in order to determine the conditions of diabetes or breathing and has its proper number. Let's examine more closely its structure and functions of the biochip on which is inscribed the so-called beast's mark or 666. The chip consists of three parts: the head, which serves as an antenna, the middle, which is a battery, and the tail, which stores various memories and many kinds of information. This information comprises 128 especially important gene memories or personal information gene memories (DNA memory codes), which modulate gene codes so that the person may be controlled not by his own thinking or will but by an outsider. In other words, the information contains such gene codes as can change the person's emotion and thinking and control his mind and will. For example, let's imagine that a certain young person graduated from a theological seminary goes to a hinterland in Africa to spread the gospel. If someone modulates his gene codes, his mind and thinking can be changed so that he may abruptly cry, "Let's worship Satan." Therefore, a man with the biochip or the beast's mark can be changed into an antichrist worshiper not by his own will but the others' (Rev. 13:8, 18).

A man with the beast's mark (666 in a biochip on his body) will be a cyborg or cybernetic organism controlled by an outsider. Antichrist can modulate the biochip code or the beast's mark of such a person so as to make him his servant. That is why we must not receive the beast's mark on our forehead or in our hand. Antichrist (αντίχριστος in Greek) is attested five times in John's Epistles (1 John 2:18, 18, 22, 4:3; 2 John 1:7). Antichrist may refer to a certain specific person (1 John 2:22, 4:3; 2 John 1:7). However, in 1 John 2:18, it is mentioned that even now, there are many antichrists. It implies that antichrist is a specific person or group. Those with the beast's mark on their body will be a worshiper of antichrist and not enter alive into the millennial kingdom but be plunged into the everlasting fire, where they will be in severe agony day and night, as is recorded in Revelation 14:9-11 and 20:4. Here, I am inclined to add something. In these last days, we must not have the beast's mark but the seal of God.

"And I saw another angel ascending from the east, having the seal of the living God: and he cried with a loud voice to the four angels, to whom it was given to hurt the earth and the sea, Saying, Hurt not the earth, neither the sea, nor the trees, till we have sealed the servants of our God in their foreheads" (Rev. 7:2-3). Since a seal stands for the ownership or authority of something, having the seal of God means belonging to God. Belonging to the Holy Spirit and God is described in John 6:27, where God the Father has sealed for the Son of man, Ephesians 1:13, where people are sealed with the Holy Spirit of promise, and Revelation 7:2, where another angel ascends from the east having the seal of the living God. Those with the seal of God will evade the great tribulation in the last days, not through their own ability or power but because they have the seal of God. The seal of God is different from the beast's mark. The seal represents a spiritual ownership while the mark is a physical token stamped on the body, which can be controlled by the beast (Rev. 13:16).

Unlike God, antichrist cannot own the souls of human beings as his own. The seal of God will be put without fail on all believers in Jesus, along with the seal of the Holy Spirit mentioned in Ephesians 1:13, at the end of this world. The seal of the Holy Spirit and the seal of God are spiritual and cannot be perceived with the naked eye. In contrast, the beast's mark or a biochip will be physically and visually infused into our right hand or forehead in the last days of this world. The seal of God will protect us from many disasters and tribulations at the end of the last days so that those sealed with God may be God's possession and cannot be killed, in such a way as the Israelites in ancient days were saved from the final plague in Egypt through the blood applied on the side posts and lintel of the door of houses, wherein they ate a lamb (Exod. 12:7, 23). Therefore, in order to survive and be remnants in the last days, we must believe in Jesus Christ and receive the seal of the Holy Spirit (Eph. 1;13, 4:30) and the seal of God put on foreheads of the last day saints just before Jesus' second coming (Rev. 7:3).

In order to let you fully know the seal of God, I want to add something here. Some contend that only 144,000 people shall receive the seal of God, citing Revelation 7:4. This turns out to be a wrong interpretation when all of Chapter 7 is carefully examined. The 144,000 people does not refer to all the saved people in this world at the end of the last days but to those saved from twelve tribes of Israel. "And I heard the number of them which were sealed: and there were sealed an hundred and forty and four thousand of all the tribes of the children of Israel" (Rev. 7:4), 12,000 from each tribe (Rev. 7:5-18). And Revelation 14:4 says, "These were redeemed from among men, being the first-fruits unto God and to the Lamb." These first-fruits are also mentioned in Jeremiah 2:3, which says, "Israel was holiness unto the LORD, and the first-fruits of his increase." The twelve tribes exclude the tribe of Dan and include those of Manasseh and Joseph. At the end of this world, not only Israelite tribes but also a great multitude, which no man could number, of all nations, kindreds, people and tongues shall be God's first-fruits (Rev. 7:9) and the servants of God shall be sealed in their foreheads (Rev. 7:3).

"After this I beheld, and, lo, a great multitude, which no man could number, of all nations, and kindreds, and people, and tongues, stood before the throne, and before the Lamb, clothed with white robes, and palms in their hands" (Rev. 7:9). At the end of this world, God's servants (Rev. 7:3) will get the seal of God, and they will include not only 144,000 people from twelve tribes of the Israel, who are first-fruits of God, but also all the Gentiles in this world, who are not first-fruits of God. A certain heresy contends that only 144,000 people shall be saved at the end of this world and we must quickly join their group before the number of 144,000 is fulfilled.

To sum up, we must not have the beast's mark at our right hand or on our forehead at the end of this world due to anti-christ's coercion. Once we get the mark, we will be controlled by antichrist (1 John 2:18) and become a cyborg and anti-christ's slave. These latter days, we should fully know and correctly understand God's word and have proper faith so that we may not receive the beast's mark but the seal of God and be survivors at the end of this world.

Eschatology

Eschatology is the doctrine of the future. In recent centuries, many people have said that the Lord's second coming was imminent. But Jesus has not yet come a second time. However, the twenty-first century or last days is really the time for the Lord's second coming. How can we know that? Very important Bible verses speak of the last days.

First, Apostle Paul tells Timothy about these latter days: "This know also, that in the last days perilous times shall come" (2 Tim. 3:1). Paul also pinpoints nineteen outstanding phenomena of the last days in 2 Timothy 3:1-5: "This know also, that in the last days perilous times shall come. For men shall be (1) lovers of their own selves, (2) covetous, (3) boasters, (4) proud, (5) blasphemers, (6) disobedient to parents, (7) unthankful, (8) unholy, (9) without natural affection, (10) truce-breakers, (11) false accusers, (12) incontinent, (13) fierce, (14) despisers of those that are good, (15) traitors, (16) heady, (17) high-minded, (18) lovers of pleasures more than lovers of God; (19) having a form of godliness, but denying the power thereof: from such turn away." Today, we are much more evidently witnessing these traits of the last days than one hundred years ago.

Second, before being crucified, Jesus taught His disciples what would happen in the last days. He said, "But of that day and hour knoweth no man, no, not the angels of heaven, but my Father only" (Matt. 24:36).

Jesus said, "And this gospel of the kingdom shall be preached in all the world for a witness unto all nations; and then shall the end come" (Matt. 24:14) and then gave a special hint as to the end of this world. "When ye therefore shall see the abomination of desolation, spoken of by Daniel the prophet, stand in the holy place, whoso readeth, let him understand" (Matt. 24:15). Why did Jesus specifically cite Daniel while mentioning the last days? It is because, of Old Testament prophets, Daniel prophesies in more detail about what happens at the end of this world. It calls for us to carefully examine the particulars of the prophecies of Daniel concerning the end of the world. Daniel 12:4 says, "But thou, O Daniel, shut up the words, and seal the book, even to the time of the end: many shall run to and fro, and knowledge shall be increased." About 2,600 years ago, Daniel prophesied "many shall run to and fro, and knowledge shall be increased" as phenomena of the latter days.

In the twenty-first century, many people run faster to and fro than in past days and have developed more knowledge and scientific civilizations. Just fifty years ago, not so many people could come and go so fast as they can today and knowledge and civilization were not developed as much as today. In 1903, for the first time in the history of human civilization, the Wright brothers flew an airplane for twelve seconds to cover only 37 meters in the air. Nowadays, however, a ships fly through space and the air.

Since 1945, computers have developed quickly. Telephone conversations can be tapped around the clock and artificial satellites in the air monitor our behaviors day and night. As Daniel prophesied, today many run to and fro and knowledge has been increased greatly. It demonstrates that today is the beginning of the end of this world.

Jesus also gives hints about the end of this world, citing verses from Daniel, including 12:11-12, "And from the time that the daily sacrifice shall be taken away, and the abomination that maketh desolate set up, there shall be a thousand two hundred and ninety days. Blessed is he that waiteth, and cometh to the thousand three hundred and five and thirty days."

According to Numbers 14:34 and Ezekiel 4:6, when interpreting prophecies in the Bible, a day is considered as one year. And according to Psalms 95:10, one generation means forty years. Daniel 11:31 records, "And arms shall stand on his part, and they shall pollute the sanctuary of strength, and shall

take away the daily sacrifice, and they shall place the abomination that maketh desolate" (see also Dan. 9:27; Matt. 24:32-
33). This verse means that the temple in Jerusalem will be de-
stroyed and replaced with the mosque called the Dome of the
Rock or the Mosque of Omar (the name of the second caliph),
which is also called the Temple of Gold. The temple was de-
stroyed on AD 70, when a Roman commander named Titus (a
son of roman emperor Vespasianus; later he became a Roman
Emperor) attacked Jerusalem. At that time, he intentionally
kept a part (now called the Wailing Wall) of the rampart un-
broken so as to display the valor of Roman soldiers who con-
quered the city wall. In the place of the temple, a mosque was
built by Abd al-Malik ibn Marwan, a successor to Muhammad,
between 685 and 691.

About four thousand years ago, Abraham nearly sacrificed his son Isaac to God (Gen. 22:9), on this site, where
later Solomon built a temple to God. In 1997 when I visited
the Temple Mount, I saw that under the dome there is a rock,
about twelve yards wide, about fifteen yards long and about two
yards high. The dome over the temple is brilliantly gold col-
ored. The Bible says that from the time that the daily sacrifice
shall be taken away and the abomination that makes desolate
set up, there shall be a thousand two hundred and ninety days,
and that blessed are the remnants that wait and come to the
thousand three hundred and five and thirty days (years) after
the establishment of the Dome of the Rock. The construction
of the Dome of the Rock was begun in 685 or 688 AD and finished in 691 AD. As for counting the last days, the Bible says of
1,260 days, 1,290 days, 1,335 days, 3.5 years, 42 months, a time,
and times and a half. So, the calculation may be developed this
way: 685+1290=1975, 685+1335=2020, or 688+1335= 2023. If it

is accepted that the Dome of the Rock was finished in 691, the calculation is 691+1335=2026.

According to Daniel 12:12, those survivors will be greatly blessed even in 1,335 years after the construction of the Dome of the Rock. What kind of blessing shall it be? It will be an unprecedented and unimaginable kind (הכרב in Hebrew). Normally, God's blessing comprises success, prosperity, wealth, honor, and multiplication of offspring, which are mentioned in Genesis 1:28 and other verses. In contrast, the blessing mentioned in Daniel 12:12 is not this kind. What is it? In Revelation, there are a blessing (μακαρίος in Greek) attested seven times (Rev. 1:3, 14:13, 16:15, 19:9, 20:6, 22:7, 22:14). Seven is the implicative perfect number. This blessing is to be given at the end of this world. Also, it is a spiritual blessing Jesus mentions while delivering the Sermon on the Mount in Matthew 5. The blessing will be given at the end of the last days stated in Daniel 12:12, during the millennium (Rev. 20:1-6) at the end of this world, in which, according to Isaiah 65, "he who dies at a hundred will be thought a mere youth; he who fails to reach a hundred will be considered accursed.... The wolf and the lamb will feed together, and the lion will eat straw like the ox, but dust will be the serpent's food" (65:20,25).

Can it happen in reality? An example is that medicine and researches into stem cells have developed so highly that various incurable diseases like cancer can often be successfully treated nowadays. It is part of the realization of the prophecies in Isaiah 65. Concerning stem cells developed by the team of Hans Robert Schöler, director of Max Planck Institute for Molecular Biomedicine in Germany, Global Trends Briefing dated June 2, 2009, reported that adult cells can be converted into one-factor induced pluripotent stem cells or that, of the four factors (Oct$_4$, Sox$_2$, Klf$_4$ and C-Myc), Oct$_4$ can be converted into a stem cells that have the same characteristics as embryo stem cells. The cell may be called a reprogrammed or an induced pluripotent stem cell, like embryo stem cells. Schöler and his teams call it iPS cell, which keeps a person growing not younger but not older and is similar to an herb of eternal youth sought after by the first emperor of China (295-210 BC) or an elixir of life by an ancient legend in China named Dong Bang-sak.

For instance, embryo stem cells extracted from the process of the generation of embryo can be divided into cells of all tissues and used to treat various diseases. In the past, a liver cancer patient needed another healthy person's liver transplanted, whose type is correspondent to his. However, today, such a person can use his own stem cells to treat his disease without any side effects. Stem cells can be applied to not only liver but also all the other internal organs for medical treatments. In more recent days when bio-ethic problems are raised, not egg cells but stem cells are used to treat diseases.

The blessing mentioned in Daniel 12:12 will be fully enjoyed around 2023 when science will be developed much more. Then, lions will not eat flesh but straw when human beings can manipulate changes in the DNA of lions. The human genome project was started in 1990 and the whole human genome was deciphered in 2003. It is expected that human genome will be fully modulated in ten years.

Genome is a compound word of gene and chromosome and refers to all the deoxyribo nucleic acids of a person. Genome gene information comprises 4 base sequences, which are listed in the order of A, T, G and C. Ninety-nine percent of about thirty trillion base sequences of a person are common to everyone and there is a difference of less than about 1 percent between individuals. The so-called custom-tailored type medical treatments may be possible since researches into genome will find out a body's physiological functions and what kinds of actions and diseases may be brought about. Modulating genes of human beings may control their emotions and thinking, and manipulating the genes of various beasts and animals may change flesh-eating animals into grass-eating ones. The time for such changes is coming to us remarkably speedily. It may possibly come true around the year of 2023 (Dan. 12:12).

To sum up, Daniel 12:12 describes changes that will take place around the year 2023, or in 1,335 years after the construction of an Islamic mosque (685 or 688) on the site of the Jerusalem temple, according to the prophecy in Isaiah 65 that a blessed world like the millennium will come. It is very clear that those surviving after 2023 will experience an unprecedented blessing of the millennial kingdom.

I want to also comment about Jesus' second coming, which will take place at the end of this world. Second Thessalonians 2:2-3 (which is also called the Pauline Apocalypse) and touches on Jesus' second coming (reincarnation) says, "not to become easily unsettled or alarmed by some prophecy, report or letter supposed to have come from us, saying that the day of the Lord has already come. Don't let anyone deceive you in any way, for that day will not come until the rebellion occurs and the man of lawlessness is revealed, the man doomed to destruction."

We should not be troubled by Jesus' second coming but remain assured that it will take place only after the appearance of the man of lawlessness (not a ghost or a spirit but a human being) who is antichrist. It is not for us to know the times or dates for Jesus' second coming the Father has set by his own authority (Acts 1:7). No one knows about that day or hour, not even the angels in heaven, nor the Son, but only the Father (see Matt. 24:36). However, we must be aware that when the man of lawlessness appears (1 John 2:22, 4:3; 2 John 1:7; Rev. 13:16-18) and the beast's mark (Rev. 13:17) is used as a means of his rule, Jesus' second coming is close at hand (2 Thess. 2:2-3; Rev. 13:15-18). Paul writes, "And do this, understanding the present time. The hour has come for you to wake up from your slumber, because our salvation is nearer now than when we first believed" (Rom. 13:11). Concerning the end of this world, Jesus says in Matthew 24:14, "And this gospel of the kingdom will be preached in the whole world as a testimony to all nations, and then the end will come."

When shall the good news of the kingdom be preached in the whole world? About a century ago, in 1910, such a thing seemed a thousand years away. Fifty years ago, it seemed to take place in four centuries away. In 1980, it seemed it might come in two hundred years. But by 2010, it was expected that within the next fifteen years the Bible will be translated and spread to all nations in the world (according to Wycliffe Bible Translators or Wycliffe's Mission 2025). Nowadays, almost every common person has a mobile phone, which was not so twenty years ago. In an African jungle or a hinterland like the Sahara Desert, people can communicate with each other by wireless phone. Moreover, as the battery for a cellular phone can be recharged through the sunlight, communication between people is much expedited. With really efficient computers, translating the Bible has been greatly enhanced. With all these measures, it is expected that spreading the gospel around the world will be accomplished by 2025.

This implies that the end of this world will come in about fifteen years. What is to be noted here is that it may be impossible for all the peoples in the world to be converted to

Christianity, but it is possible for the gospel to be propagated into each corner of the world. The former is totally different from the latter. The end of the world will come not when all the people around the world have been evangelized but when all the people around the world have heard the gospel (the Bible). Now, it is good for us, the remnant people, to live even after 2023 and be surprisingly blessed with God's favor. Daniel says, "As for you, go your way till the end. You will rest, and then at the end of the days you will rise to receive your allotted inheritance" (12:13). Resurrection (Rev. 20:12) refers to a sudden metamorphosis into a spiritual body (Matt. 24:40-41; 1 Cor. 15:44, 15:52; 1 Thess. 4:16-17) and a rapture into the air at the end of the last days after the second coming of Jesus, in such a manner as Enoch (Gen. 5:24) and Elijah (2 Kings 2:11) ascended to heaven. Paul says, "Listen, I tell you a mystery: We will not all sleep, but we will all be changed in a flash, in the twinkling of an eye, at the last trumpet. For the trumpet will sound, the dead will be raised imperishable, and we will be changed" (1 Cor. 15:51-52). Those who do not change and die at the last trumpet will be resurrected after the millennial kingdom in order to be judged before the white throne.

A change from the natural body into a resurrection body may be compared to that from a pupa to a butterfly, for "there is a natural body and there is a spiritual body" (1 Cor. 15:44). When Jesus comes again to the earth and the millennial kingdom is set up (Rev. 20:4-6), the residents of the kingdom will include those martyrs who have come along with Jesus and participate in the first resurrection (Rev. 20:4), those who will have been suddenly changed into a spiritual body (1 Thess. 4:17), and those who will have not received the beast's mark on the earth (Rev. 20:4,6). Those who participate in the first resurrection will no longer die since they will be equal unto the angels

(Luke 20:36; Rom. 6:9; Rev. 21:4) nor be resurrected over again (Rev. 20:4-8). And they will neither marry nor be given in marriage (Matt. 22:30, Mark 12:25, Luke 20:35). "For when they shall rise from the dead, they neither marry, nor are given in marriage; but are as the angels which are in heaven" (Mark 12:25). After battles in Gog (Eze. 38:3) and Magog (Rev. 20:8) and the Satan, the beast, and the false prophet are thrown alive into the fiery lake of burning sulfur (Rev. 19:20, 20:10), those who have not attended the first resurrection will all be resurrected (John 5:28-29; Acts 24:15; 1 Cor. 15:52; Rev. 20:12) and changed into a special body or resurrection body to be judged (Rev. 20:11) before God's great white throne (2 Cor. 5:10; Rev. 20:13). The resurrection body will be like what it was on this earth: it will be a child when it died a child or a sound body even if it died crippled (1 Sam. 28:14; Matt. 17:3; Luke 9:30).

When they are resurrected, those having committed many dreadful sins in this world but believed in Christ and repented their sins will rise to live (John 5:29), be made perfect (Heb. 12:23) and enter the kingdom of heaven. Another person, who has not lived a bad life in this world and whom people praise as "honest" and "good" but who has not believed in Jesus Christ nor had his original sin has been forgiven, he shall rise to be condemned (John 5:29) and plunged not into the lake of burning sulfur but hell or the lake of fire (Rev. 20:14), where his immortal body shall not die but be in everlasting torture (Mark 9:48-49; Luke 20:36). Whether they are in Hades or paradise after death, all spirits which have a resurrection body will be put to judgment without exception (John 5:29; Acts 24:15; Rev. 20:12-13). Not our corruptible blood and flesh but our resurrection body will go to heaven. Concerning this, Paul says in 1 Corinthians 15:50, "I declare to you, brothers, that flesh and blood cannot inherit the kingdom of God, nor does the perishable inherit the imperishable."

Resurrection will take place only once (Rev. 20:6) and is totally different from revival. A revived body will once again get old or diseased. Jesus revived Lazarus (John 11:1-44), a daughter of Jairus (Matt. 5:22), and a son of a widow in Nain (Luke 7:11-17), all of whom later died once again. Dead were raised alive by not only Jesus but also by Elijah (1 Kings 17:17-24), Elisha (2 Kings 4:32-35), Peter (Acts 9:37-40), and Paul (Acts 20:9-10), but all of the revived persons later died once again. In contrast, the resurrection body is immortal (Luke 20:36; Rom. 6:9; 1 Cor. 15:54; Rev. 20:6, 21:4). Such a body can see both visible material things and invisible spiritual things; it can see the past and future of the physical world, in the same way as the dead rich person saw the dead beggar Lazarus in Luke 16.

The special resurrection body will not age or decay (1 Cor. 15:42, 54) but transcend the boundaries of time and space (John 20:19-26; Luke 24:31). The resurrection body can go from one corner of the earth to another in no time (Luke 24:31) and penetrate even into a locked strongbox (John 20:19). The resurrection body is not limited in terms of space since it is a spiritual being. And it can eat roasted fish (Gen. 18:1-8, 19:3; John 21:9-13), stay alive for a long time without eating anything (Rev. 7:16), and will not marry nor be given in marriage but be like angels (Matt. 22:30; Mark 12:25) since it is a special body (1 Cor. 15:44). What is the difference in the body between before its resurrection and after resurrection? Before resurrection, the body grows, ages, sickens, and dies because it is a material, mortal, and natural body. In contrast, after resurrection, the body will never again age, sicken, or pass away but permanently exist. Unlike a natural body (σώμα φυσικόν in Greek), the resurrection body is controlled by the spirit (1

Cor. 15:44). Unlike a ghost, the resurrection or spiritual body (σῶμα πνευματικόν in Greek) has flesh (Luke 24:37-43; John 20:27) and can eat something (1 Cor. 15:44). Why does the resurrection body not grow old, aged or exhausted as time goes by? Because the resurrection body does not belong to the material world but to the non-material world and the spiritual invisible realm. Since Christ rose from the dead and became the first-fruit of them that slept (1 Cor. 15:20), we will also be resurrected in such a way. As Jesus ascended with the clouds to heaven in a resurrection body (Acts 1:11), at the end of this world, He will come in a resurrection body again down to this world along with angels (Rev. 1:7; Matt. 16:27, 26:64; Luke 9:26; Dan. 7:13). Since it is immortal or invulnerable (Luke 20:36; Rev. 20:6) like angels, the resurrection body can never die again nor be burned away in the lake of fire (Matt. 18:8-9; Mark 9:48-49) but will be everlastingly tortured if appropriate. The resurrection body will live permanently (Phil. 3:21) since only humans have the spirit, which does not die at all once it is created (Luke 20:36; Rev. 21:4).

Suicide
Suicide, which I call self-murder, is much discussed today. Statistics say that about one million people around the world kill themselves each year. The World Health Organization observes September 10 each year as the world suicide-prevention day. From the Christian point of view, there are three important perspectives on suicide.

First, many people seem to think that once they leave this world through suicide, all of their problems will be disconnected from them because they will return to nothing after death. Many are persuaded that there is no other way to solve their problems than to kill themselves. From this standpoint,

Christianity has a different perspective. It believes that once a man is born into this world, his flesh shall age, sicken, and pass away while his spirit will never die or decay. Even though a man can kill his own body, he cannot do so to his spirit, which is the core of his being (Luke 16:23). When one dies, the spirit, which is immaterial, is separated from the body, which is material. Death is not permanent passing-away; just a separation of material from immaterial.

What is more startling is that the spirit cannot die; it exists even after the flesh has passed away. After death, the spiritual body leaves this world and suffers everlasting torture in the everlasting world. What we must realize is that when we commit suicide we cannot totally exterminate our whole being; we kill our body only because we still have the spirit. This fact is forgotten or not known by self-murderers. So, their wrong thinking or misunderstanding leads to a great mistake. In this world, there is a miracle: a crisis may turn into an opportunity and bad luck often brings good luck. Jeremiah 18:6 records, "O house of Israel, cannot I do with you as this potter? saith the LORD. Behold, as the clay is in the potter's hand, so are ye in mine hand, O house of Israel." We need to wait and see that all things work together for the good of those who love God and are the called according to his purpose (Rom. 8:28).

Second, it is the same sin for us to kill ourselves as to kill other people since all creation is the possession of God. Psalms 24:1 says, "The earth is the LORD's, and the fullness thereof; the world, and they that dwell therein." Isaiah 43:1 says, "thou art mine." All property and wealth, including the life of humans, are owned by God the Creator. Humans are no more than a manager or steward of them. Common unbelievers try not to destroy their own body since they believe that their hair and skin are inherited from and a possession of their parents.

Buddhists believe that suicide is the same heinous wrongdoing as killing others and leads men into the deepest hell. Self-murder is a kind of murder and a sin regardless of the reasons.

Third, the ultimate goal of Christians is going to heaven after death. Christianity clearly teaches that people go to heaven after death if their sins are forgiven or to hell if they remain sinners. A murderer can go to heaven if he repents of his wrongdoing, believes in Jesus, and his sins are forgiven. But after death, a self-murderer cannot repent of his wrongdoing or suicide because an opportunity will not be given for him to do so in the next world. Therefore, those committing suicide on any ground and not repenting of their sins will be plunged into everlasting hellfire (Matt. 27:5). The same applies to believers and unbelievers since the Bible says, "For it is impossible for those who were once enlightened, and have tasted of the heavenly gift, and were made partakers of the Holy Ghost and have tasted the good word of God, and the powers of the world to come. If they shall fall away, to renew them again unto repentance; seeing they crucify to themselves the Son of God afresh, and put him to an open shame" (Heb. 6:4-6), and "For if we sin wilfully after that we have received the knowledge of the truth, there remaineth no more sacrifice for sins, But a certain fearful looking for of judgment and fiery indignation, which shall devour the adversaries" (Heb. 10:26-27).

Conflicts in the Church
It is clear that any conflict among church members comes from Satan since the fruit of the Spirit is love, joy, peace, longsuffering, gentleness, goodness, faith and others (Gal. 5:22), and the Holy Spirit never works through evil conflicts or disputes. If there is a conflict in the church, it is evident that one or both parties of the conflict belong to evil. Galatians 5:19-21

records, "Now the works of the flesh are manifest, which are these; adultery, fornication, uncleanness, lasciviousness, idolatry, witchcraft, hatred, variance, emulations, wrath, strife, seditions, heresies, envying, murders, drunkenness, revellings, and such like: of the which I tell you before, as I have also told you in time past, that they which do such things shall not inherit the kingdom of God." When there are conflicts among church members for any reason, Satan rejoices greatly (John 8:44).

About fifty years ago, there was a family with two sons and one daughter. Next door, there was another family, whose head was an army captain. Her mother gave a new skirt to the daughter, who wanted to strut it to the next door housewife. The daughter agreed to exchange her skirt with the shoes of the housewife. However, the family of the daughter did not approve the deal. So, she asked the housewife to make the deal void. But the housewife rejected it. Soon, there was a big battle between the two families, which led to the death of the captain caused by the second son of the opponent family striking him with a club. Three years later, the mother of the son became sick due to a mental or emotional disorder as a result of her repressed anger or stress since her son was put into prison. This story shows that a small strife may lead to a big battle, which will possibly bring about unexpected results.

Here is another story that happened forty years ago in New York. A Jew ran a store, where a group of boys would make fun of the shop owner every day. One day the owner gave a half dollar, which was big money at that time to them, to each of the boys. Next day, he gave a quarter to each. The next day ten cents and the following day five cents.

The following day, he said to them, "Boys, I do not have any money to offer you more." Then, they would not come to the store any more. Why? Their purpose to come to the store was lost. At first, they did not come for the money, but later they did. It implies that the initial purpose for starting a strife may be changed at last depending on the thoughts or conditions of the persons concerned.

James 4:1 says, "From whence come wars and fights among you? come they not hence, even of your lusts that war in your members?" Lusts do not come from the Holy Spirit but from Satan. Therefore, a battle or strife in the church or God's house does come from not the Holy Spirit but lusts brought on by evil or devil. It is very clear that one or both of the parties of a battle belong to the devil.

When such battles takes place, we must take time for self-examination and consider if we have not been in a snare of the devil. "Moreover, [we] must have a good report of them which are without; lest he we into reproach and the snare of the devil" (1 Tim. 3:7). We must "in meekness instruct those that oppose themselves" so that, "if God peradventure will give them repentance to the acknowledging of the truth, they may recover themselves out of the snare of the devil, who are taken captive by him at his will" (2 Tim. 2:25,26). This is an essential instrument for winning a spiritual battle. Each of us must be made sacred and sanctified in order not fall into the snare of Satan.

Let's carefully consider the story of the fall of Jericho recorded in Joshua 5. When Moses got up unto mount Nebo, which is in the land of Moab and over against Jericho, after he led Israel out of Egypt, he died and Joshua was appointed as a new leader of Israel (Deut. 34:1-5). Israel was making every effort to conquer Jericho, which was an impregnable fortress. "And it came to pass, when Joshua was by Jericho, that he lifted up his eyes and looked, and, behold, there stood a man over against him with his sword drawn in his hand: and Joshua went unto him, and said unto him, Art thou for us, or for our adversaries? And he said, Nay; but as captain of the host of the LORD am I now come. And Joshua fell on his face to the earth, and did worship, and said unto him, What saith my Lord unto his servant? And the captain of the Lord's host said unto Joshua, Loose thy shoe from off thy foot, for the place whereon you stand is holy. And Joshua did so" (Josh. 5:13-15).

This story informs us that we should consider if we are siding with Satan or God, since we should not stand with Satan but in a holy place in order to get assistance from the host of the LORD (Josh. 5:14). First Chronicles 18 draws our attention to the showdown between Prophet Elijah and 850 false prophets for Baal. In verse 21, Elijah hurled words of thunder at Israel, "How long halt ye between two opinions? if the LORD be God, follow him: but if Baal, then follow him. And the people answered him not a word." So, we must be separated from evil and stand with God Jehovah. And we must "be not overcome of evil, but overcome evil with good" (Rom. 12:21) "for we wrestle not against flesh and blood, but against principalities, against powers, against the rulers of the darkness of this world, against spiritual wickedness in high places" (Eph. 6:12).

In order to defeat evil, we must not fight with human effort but with God's almighty power (Josh. 5:13-14; Judg. 7:22; 2 Chr. 20:22; 1 Sam. 14:28). The impregnable fortress of Jericho fell through using not any human power, when Israel went round the fortress for seven days while led by the ark of covenant. Chapter 6 of Judges and the following chapters describe a story of Gideon and his three hundred warriors. Thirty-two thousand Israelites were ready to fight with one hundred thirty-five thousand Midianite soldiers. However, Jehovah ordered Gideon to reduce the number of the Israelites. When twenty-two thousand went back and only ten thousand remained, God said there were still too many. "And the LORD said unto

Gideon, By the three hundred men that lapped from the water will I save you, and deliver the Midianites into thine hand: and let all the other people go every man unto his place" (Jud. 7:7). The three hundred Israelites were not good at war but just lapped up water. They did not have good weapons, only trumpets, pitchers, and lamps.

It was very evident that the battle would not be won by Israelites, since they were faced with so many enemies. Yet the Bible says that the three hundred warriors of Gideon could defeat their enemies when the Israelites relied not on human power but on the works of the Holy Spirit (Judges 8:10).

Second Kings 6 tells the story of the Syrian king who sent soldiers to capture Elisha an Israelite prophet. In the morning, a servant of Elisha found Syrian soldiers swarming. He told Elisha that Aramaic soldiers were coming to take him. Elisha answered, "Fear not: for they that be with us are more than they that be with them. And Elisha prayed, and said, LORD, I pray thee, open his eyes, that he may see. And the LORD opened the eyes of the young man; and he saw: and, behold, the mountain was full of horses and chariots of fire round about Elisha. And when they came down to him, Elisha prayed unto the LORD, and said, Smite this people, I pray thee, with blindness. And he smote them with blindness according to the word of Elisha. And Elisha said unto them, This is not the way, neither is this the city: follow me, and I will bring you to the man whom ye seek. But he led them to Samaria. And it came to pass, when they were come into Samaria, that Elisha said, LORD, open the eyes of these men, that they may see. And the LORD opened their eyes, and they saw; and, behold, they were in the midst of Samaria. And the king of Israel said unto Elisha, when he saw them, My father, shall I smite them? shall I smite them? And he answered, Thou shalt not smite them. Wouldest thou smite those whom thou hast taken captive with thy sword and with thy bow? Set bread and water before them, that they may eat and drink, and go to their master" (2 King 6:16-22).

These stories show that we cannot beat off the devil with our power but with the power of the Holy Spirit only. In order to win such a spiritual battle or get help from God's soldiers, we need incessantly present intercessions, especially united intercessory prayers. In a spiritual fight, we can reject Satan's temptations through our fervent prayers. With our might, knowledge, or power, we can only recompense evil for evil. The Bible says, "Recompense to no man evil for evil. Provide things honest in the sight of all men" (Rom. 12:17). "See that none render evil for evil unto any man; but ever follow that which is good, both among yourselves, and to all men" (1 Thess. 5:15). The life of Christians is materialized when bearing the cross, "for all the law is fulfilled in one word, even in this; Thou shalt love thy neighbour as thyself. But if ye bite and devour one another, take heed that ye be not consumed one of another" (Gal. 5:14-15). Peter also says, "Not rendering evil for evil, or railing for railing: but contrariwise blessing; knowing that ye are thereunto called, that ye should inherit a blessing" (1 Pet. 3:9). Paul says, "And let us not be weary in well doing: for in due season we shall reap, if we faint not" (Gal. 6:9).

Defeating evil with the Holy Spirit's works, we will see that all things work together for good to them that love God, to them who are the called according to his purpose. After he killed his younger brother Abel, "the LORD said unto Cain, Where is Abel thy brother? And he said, I know not: Am I my brother's keeper? And Abel, he also brought of the firstlings of his flock and of the fat thereof. And the LORD had respect unto Abel and to his offering: but unto Cain and to his offering he had not respect. And Cain was very wroth, and his countenance fell. And the LORD said unto Cain, Why art thou wroth? And why is thy countenance fallen? If thou doest well, shalt thou not be accepted? And if thou doest not well, sin lies at the door. And unto thee shall be his desire, and thou shalt rule over him. And Cain talked with Abel his brother: and it came to pass, when they were in the field, that Cain rose up against Abel his brother, and slew him. And the LORD said unto Cain, Where is Abel thy brother? And he said, I know not: Am I my brother's keeper?" (Gen. 4:6-9). What comes from evil can never be the works of the Spirit but of the devil.

King David raped Bathsheba the wife of Uriah and she became pregnant. Then, the prophet Nathan visited the king and blamed him. David did not order the arrest of the prophet but confessed his own sin (2 Sam. 12:13). David did not fly into a rage like Cain but repented his sin and evil under the influence of the Holy Spirit. Some church members get angry when they are scolded for their wrongdoing. That is not a work of the Holy Spirit.

Christians should not flare up at a scold or admonition like Cain did but sincerely repent of their sins or wrongdoing like David. Wherever Satan is active, discord and conflicts occur. In contrast, wherever the Holy Spirit is active, there will concord, peace, and joy only. In a harmonious and peaceful family, members will not get enraged when blamed or scolded against wrongdoing like Cain and will fall into reproach and the snare of the devil but, like David, will regret the wrongdoing under the influence of the Holy Spirit so that the family may be filled with prayers for love, joy, and peace (2 Cor. 5:17).

In explaining the resurrection body, I will briefly touch on time and space defined by modern science. Light moves 297,600 kilometers a second. They say that light runs round the earth 7.5 times a second, which is 300,000 kilometers or three trillion meters. Tachyon is speedier than the light. The theory of tachyon (ταχιον in Greek), which is a hypothetical subatomic particle that moves faster than light, was first introduced in a thesis presented in 1967 by Gerald Feinberg, a professor of physics in Columbia University. And the theory of chronon was advanced in 1982 by David Finkelstein a professor of physics in Georgia Institute of Technology. Chronon is a quantum of time or a discrete and indivisible unit of time proposed by the theory, which assumes that time is not continuous.

In Greek, which is the original language of the New Testament, there are two kinds of time: καιρός and χρόνος. χρόνος is a general concept of time, which is chronological, quantitative and human time (Acts 7:17; Heb. 5:12; Rev. 2:21). In contrast, καιρός refers to qualitative and divine time determined in God's providence (Num. 23:23; Eccl. 3:11; Dan. 2:21; Matt. 13:30; John 7:6, 8). The Greek word ώρα is used many times in John's Gospel and means the time for Jesus' second coming (Matt. 24:36; Mark 13:42) or for a human promise, like a wedding time. The concept of time can be established only when space exists. Physical and human time in this material world is χρόνος while καιρός is divine time in the spiritual or non-material world where there is no normal time and space.

The theories of relativity, as advanced by Albert Einstein, assume that time runs according to space and very slowly in spaces like a black hole. Therefore, in the vast universe, there is no absolute time as on the earth but relative time, which runs quickly or slowly depending on conditions. Relative time runs in a different speed depending on conditions of the space, which is called the super-space or hyper-space by physicists, or also called the space of Euclid (a Greek mathematician living in c. 300 BC). This is a theoretical space where three-dimensional space converges into a point.

The third heaven Paul describes (2 Cor. 12:2-4) does not belong to what we know as the universe but it is beyond the universe, where super light and super space exist. It is a place where there are the paradise Paul witnessed and the white throne (Rev. 20:11) witnessed by John. This is called in the Bible "the heaven and the heaven of heavens" (Deut. 10:14) or "the heaven and heaven of heavens" (1 Kings 8:27; 2 Chr. 2:6; Neh. 9:6), which comprise the first heaven or the atmospheric heaven, the second heaven or the universe, and the third heaven beyond the universe. At the time of the final judgment before the white throne, this universe and this earth, or the first heaven and the first earth, will pass away and there will be a new heaven and a new earth (Rev. 21:1).

It seems that Indians applied the theory of chronon in ancient days when they divided one second into trillion time protons. Time proton is a concept of time corpuscle, which transcends light particles or photons and the spaces of the current universe. The Bible says, "For a thousand years in thy sight are but as yesterday when it is past, and as a watch in the night" (Ps. 90:4) and "one day is with the Lord as a thousand years, and a thousand years as one day" (2 Pet. 3:8). If we cold live in the hyper-space where the super light speed is applied, we would not get old and aged. I think such a divine super space is part of heaven and hell and that resurrection bodies live in the super space. A conclusion of the doctrine of man is that all animals have flesh and a soul while only human beings, the lord of all creation, have the spirit.

The spirit is a nonmaterial thing God the Creator has specially given to human beings only, and it will not die but exist permanently either in heaven or hell after the last judgment. From the beginning, men have an image of God or the conscience, which has been lost (depraved) since Adam and Eve ate the fruit of the tree of knowledge and has become the so-called conscience seared with a hot iron and leads men separated from God to death (Gen. 2:17, 3:19). Human beings often ask these questions: From where did I come and to where shall I go? What brought me here to this world? What am I? In order to understand who we are, we must first understand who God the Creator is. As a watch is not made accidentally but purposefully, so we are by God the Creator. The purpose of the creation of us is revealed and disclosed in God's word. Knowing God the Creator, we can realize that secular power and material richness are infinitely vain and men are dreadful and evil sinners if they are not given forgiveness of their sins, which lead to death (Job 42:5-6).

God has made us not beasts but human with the spirit. He saved and adopted us as His children, who can enjoy everlasting life and give glory to God. Then, how can we be God's children and enjoy everlasting life? In order for us to recover God's image, which is lost, we must believe in Jesus Christ and our sins forgiven through Jesus Christ's blood. The Holy Spirit must dwell in us so that we may be born again and grafted in (Rom. 8:9; 11:17). The grafting cannot be made by our effort or power but by the hand of Jehovah God only. Through God's gift (Eph. 2:8), grace and favor, we can recover the lost image and call God Abba or Father (Rom. 8:16; Gal. 4:6; Jer. 3:19). Unless we are changed (transformed) or born again, and unless the Holy Spirit and Jesus Christ dwell in us and we have the resurrection faith, we can never live a perfect life as a Christian (Rom. 8:9).

What is the difference between regret and repentance? Regret is deploring and lamenting our wrongdoing, while repenting is deploring and lamenting our wrongdoing plus determining to do it never again. For example, one who regrets his drunkenness may think that it is wrong and blame himself for it. In contrast, one who repents his drunkenness pledges himself he will drink never again since drinking may lead to a big accident. Jesus does not tell to regret but to repent (Matt. 4:17; Mark 1:15). Unlike regret, repentance can never be late but always lead to good fruit. True repentance will lead to the change or transformation of life since repentance is a change of mind brought about by the Holy Spirit. Jesus warns us, "except ye repent, ye shall all likewise perish" (Luke 13:5). There are many differences between sensual natural men and reborn spiritual men. The greatest difference is that reborn Christians can repent of their sins and reflect themselves while natural men can not.

The greatest sins include not murder and robbery but pride, which is hated and disliked the most by God. Second Kings 5 describes the story of Naaman, a leper and a captain of the host of the king of Syria. When he came to Elisha in order to get his disease healed, he was told to go to the Jordan River and wash seven times. In response, Naaman became enraged "and said, 'Behold, I thought, He will surely come out to me, and stand, and call on the name of the LORD his God, and strike his hand over the place, and recover the leper.'" As he turned and went away in a rage, his servants came near and spake unto him, and said, "if the prophet had bid thee do some great thing, wouldest thou not have done it? how much rather then, when he saith to thee, Wash, and be clean?" So, when he obeyed the command of the Israelite prophet, his leprosy was completely cured. This story tells us that not pride but humility leads to salvation. Naaman was a high ranking person and his high status could not heal his sickness, but his modesty could do so. Pride came from comparing oneself with others and humility comes from comparing oneself with God, who loves and cares for an obscure person like me.

We can be truly humble when we carefully consider not only what happens around us but also recognize the presence of God the Creator, who makes that happen. In order to be condescending, we must always pray for that and not compare ourselves with others but with God the Almighty, like Job. In Job 42:5-6, he says, "I have heard of thee by the hearing of the ear: but now mine eye seeth thee. Wherefore I abhor myself, and repent in dust and ashes." We can truly be humble when we perceive our iniquities and sins since "If we say that we have no sin, we deceive ourselves, and the truth is not in us" (1 John 1:8). Being humble will result in a prosperous and blessed life since "By humility and the fear of the LORD are riches, and honour, and life" (Prov. 22:4) and "For thus saith the high and lofty One that inhabiteth eternity, whose name is Holy; I dwell in the high and holy place, with him also that is of a contrite and humble spirit, to revive the spirit of the humble, and to revive the heart of the contrite ones" (Isa. 57:15).

"For all those things hath mine hand made, and all those things have been, saith the LORD: but to this man will I look, even to him that is poor and of a contrite spirit, and trembleth at my word" (Isa. 66:2). According to the Bible, God's people including Isaac, Jacob, Joseph, Moses, Joshua, and even Jesus Christ can lead a victorious life when God is with them (Gen. 26:24, 28:15, 39:23; Exod. 3:12; Josh. 1:5; John 8:16, 29, 16:32). To be a winner, we should also get along with God. We are blessed when we have a good mentor. We are the most blessed in the world when we have Immanuel as our mentor and when we are filled with the Holy Spirit and walk with God. When we walk with God, we are and can be blessed by Jehovah God, who is our Lord and the source of all good fortunes, as is stated in Philippines 4:9, "Those things, which ye have both learned, and received, and heard, and seen in me, do: and the God of peace shall be with you" (Gen. 12:12, Deut. 11:26, Prov. 10:22). When we are humble, we give thanks to God for everything. When are thankful to God, we are obedient to God. When we are not thankful to God, we are disobedient to God and dissatisfied and discontented with Him. Believers are expected to be thankful for everything. Our happiness and thankfulness are not dependent upon the quantities of possessions but on our thinking or feeling. Happiness is not absolute but relative, considering 2 Corinthians 2:16 which says, "To the one we are the savior of death unto death; and to the other the savior of life unto life. And who is sufficient for these things?" So, our happiness and thanks are never directly given by God but derived from response to our surroundings. God bestows on us while happiness and thanks are dependent on our attitude of mind. This implies that the source of happiness is different from that of blessing. Thanksgiving people are happy people. As blow flies swarm about an ill smell and bees and butterflies flock around fragrant flowers, so evil will come together where there is discontent and dissatisfaction.

Even when we give thanks against our will, our sweet thanksgiving invites angels to help us (1 Cor. 2:16). There is no thanksgiving where discontent and dissatisfied people live and evil exists. In any condition and environment, you can find either a cause for discontent or for thanksgiving. We will be prosperous in everything if we are thankful for everything. Thanksgiving makes the difference between live faith and dead faith. We are not truly thankful when we forget Jehovah God the Creator who controls everything happening in our life (1 Sam. 2:6-7; 1

Chr. 29:11-12) and when we are not self-sufficient but boastful. It is why the Bible says, "Pride goeth before destruction, and an haughty spirit before a fall" (Prov. 16:18). Haughty persons can never be thankful since pride leads to conflict and discord and humility to peace and concord.

Conclusion

As a conclusion of the doctrine of man, we need to consider how we should spend the remainder of our life. Christians should react correctly and rightly to God, people and materials. To do that, we must recognize that we are creatures and always keep in mind the Bible verse, "Prepare to meet your God" (Amos 4:12) before the white throne of judgment.

The conclusion of this book is that the cores of Christianity are the salvation derived from the cross and the eternal life from resurrection. Jesus the Son of God was crucified in order to execute God's righteousness, and Jesus was resurrected in order to demonstrate God's love. Therefore, Christianity, if it does not lead to the salvation derived from the cross and the eternal life from resurrection, is totally meaningless and useless. The essential doctrines of Christianity include the salvation given on the cross of Jesus Christ and the eternal life of resurrection body. As "we know that all things work together for good to them that love God, to them who are the called according to his purpose" (Rom. 8:28), God's children should lead their life in a positive manner while being assured that all things work together for good in God's love. For the rest of our days, we must believe that Jesus Christ is our savior, the way, truth and life; hope that the crown of our glory is prepared for us in the kingdom of heaven; and labor in love to bear our cross and do our best in this world to receive salvation.

APPENDIX 1

Hardships

"I have heard of thee by the hearing of the ear: but now mine eye seeth thee" (Job 42:5).

We will be faced with tribulations and adversities, difficulties and troubles, small or big, in this world. What kinds of lessons are such tribulations and difficulties to provide us with and how should we respond to such difficulties? The answer can be derived from the experiences of Job.

Historicity of the Story of Job
The Bible says that Job really existed and his story is also true. Uz (Job 1:1; Lam. 4:21) was a fertile tract of Edom in the borderland with Egypt south of the Dead Sea (Job 1:14). Job really existed in history and his name is mentioned in Genesis 46:13, which records, "And the sons of Issachar; Tola, and Phuvah, and Job, and Shimron." The name is also stated in 1 Chronicles 7:1, which records, "Now the sons of Issachar were, Tola, and Puah, Jashub, and Shimrom, four," where Job is referred to as Jashub. Issachar, Job's father, is the fifth son of Leah, Jacob's first wife (Gen. 35:23). It is very sure that Job really existed in history since Ezekiel 14:14 records, "Though these three men, Noah, Daniel, and Job were in it, they should deliver but their own

souls by their righteousness, saith the Lord GOD." According to the Bible, Eliphaz the Temanite, a friend of Job, is the first son of Esau (Gen. 36:4) and the father of Teman (Gen. 36:11). Bildad the Shuhite is also a friend of Job. Shuah, a friend of Job, is the sixth son of Keturah, Abraham's second wife (Gen. 25:2; 1 Chr. 1:32). Zophar the Naamathite (Gen. 36:20, 29; 1 Chr. 1:40) is also a friend of Job and a grandson of Esau.

All of Job's friends mentioned in the Bible are his relatives. Therefore, Job lived in the time when sons or grandsons of Esau and Jacob lived. Carefully considering the last chapter, which records that, when Job lived a hundred and forty years more, he was blessed twice as much as he had before (Job 42:10), it is estimated that Job was around 70 years old when the story takes place. During his tribulation, Job says, "Now they that are younger than I have me in derision" (Job 30:1), which implies that Job was not thirty or forty years old at that time but very old because he already had ten grown children (Job 1:2). Job's friends said to Job, "With us are both the gray-headed and very aged men, much elder than thy father" (Job 15:10). The gray-headed is Eliphaz, who was more than 140 years old at that time. So, Job was about seventy.

Job was in torture not for years but for a few months, since Job 7:3 records, "So am I made to possess months of vanity, and wearisome nights are appointed to me." It seems that Job's friends did not stay for a long time with Job for consolation.

Cause for Job's Torture
Job's tribulation was not caused by his wrongdoing or sin. Job 1:1 says, "There was a man in the land of Uz, whose name was Job; and that man was perfect and upright, and one that feared God, and eschewed evil." In Job 2:3, "the LORD said unto Satan, Hast thou considered my servant Job, that there is

none like him in the earth, a perfect and an upright man, one that feareth God, and escheweth evil? and still he holdeth fast his integrity, although thou movedst me against him, to destroy him without cause."

Job did not commit a great sin once grown up since he says to God, "For thou writest bitter things against me, and makest me to possess the iniquities of my youth" (Job 13:26). Job's friends said to him, "Know therefore that God exacteth of thee less than thine iniquity deserveth" (Job 11:6). In response, he said to them, "Teach me, and I will hold my tongue: and cause me to understand wherein I have erred" (Job 6:24), which implies that he had never committed a blunder.

Satan's Wickedness

Job suffered torture and tribulation purely because of Satan sarcastically provoked God to anger (Job 1:8, 2:3). "Satan answered the LORD, and said, Doth Job fear God for naught? Hast not thou made an hedge about him, and about his house, and about all that he hath on every side? Thou hast blessed the work of his hands, and his substance is increased in the land" (Job 1:9-10). So, in order to prove the integrity of the heart of Job, God unwillingly permitted Satan to strike Job. At first, God allowed Satan to put his hand on Job's possessions only (Job 1:12), not his body. Job's tribulation and torture were not caused by his iniquities or sins but by Satan's tricks.

Job's Hardships

Job said, "Naked came I out of my mother's womb, and naked shall I return thither: the LORD gave, and the LORD hath taken away; blessed be the name of the LORD. In all this Job sinned not, nor charged God foolishly" (Job 1:21-22).

In chapter 2, Satan once again ridiculed God's word: "Skin for skin, yea, all that a man hath will he give for his life" (Job 2:4).

At this, God permitted Satan to strike Job but not put his hand on Job's life (Job 2:6). "So went Satan forth from the presence of the LORD, and smote Job with sore boils from the sole of his foot unto his crown. And he took him a potsherd to scrape himself withal; and he sat down among the ashes. Then said his wife unto him, Dost thou still retain thine integrity? Curse God, and die. But he said unto her, Thou speakest as one of the foolish women speaketh. What? shall we receive good at the hand of God, and shall we not receive evil? In all this did not Job sin with his lips (Job 2:7-10).

Verbal Mistakes

It is very important for us not to make verbal mistakes. The Bible says, "For in many things we offend all. If any man offend not in word, the same is a perfect man, and able also to bridle the whole body" (James 3:2). Often times, many people, especially high-ranking persons, are forced from office due to their verbal mistakes. How can we not make such mistakes? We can do so through stopping our mouth securely and considering the following testing stones.

First, we must consider whether what we are going to say is true. If it is true, then okay. Second, we must consider whether what we are going to tell is useful or beneficial to the listener(s). For example, when you are giving a good tip for the safety of a traveler, you are telling a useful thing. Third, in any meeting, there are many people who want to speak, a few people who desire to be opinion leaders, or some unwilling to speak the truth because they will be disadvantaged, disliked, or suppressed. The last ones are "dumb dogs" mentioned in

Isaiah 56:10. If there is no one to speak the truth, I myself will tell it; and this is a good determination.

Fourth, we must consider the effects of what we are going to tell, since a small fire may grow into a big one. We need to remain silent if what we are going to tell will possibly have a great negative effect. Fifth, we should remember that, when we stand before God sitting on the white throne of judgment (Matt. 12:36-37), we must account for everything we say because all liars shall have their part in the lake which burns with fire and brimstone (Rev. 21:8, 27, 22:15).

Lie are of two kinds: telling there is something when there is not, or vice versa. One is exaggeration and the other is abridgment. In Acts 5, Ananias and his wife sold their possessions, then brought the money and laid it at the apostles' feet. But they kept back part of the proceeds. At this, Peter became angry and said, "Ananias, why hath Satan filled thine heart to lie to the Holy Ghost, and to keep back part of the price of the land? Whiles it remained, was it not thine own? and after it was sold, was it not in thine own power? why hast thou conceived this thing in thine heart? thou hast not lied unto men, but unto God. And Ananias hearing these words fell down, and gave up the ghost" (Acts 5:3-5).

There is the story in Joshua 2 of Rahab the harlot, who hid two Israelite spies on the roof of her house and amid stalks of flax. Then, she lied and told Jericho's soldiers that the spies had just left and could be caught if the soldiers followed quickly.

In general, such a lie in an inescapable case is not allowed either, since death and life are in the power of the tongue: and they that love it shall eat the fruit thereof (Prov. 18:21). Often, a word of encouragement or praise leads a discouraged person to a success or prosperity.

If the five testing stones mentioned above—what you are going to say is true; it will be useful to the listener; only you can say it; you know the effects of what you are saying; and you remember that you shall stand before the final judgment seat—have been all been checked, then you can say what you have in your mind. If you apply and practice these five rules, you can usually avoid verbal mistakes.

In the days of Job, Satan was still in heaven before the throne of God (Job 1:6-7, 2:1-2) and would freely come and go before God. I think that Satan was thrown down from heaven to this earth (or the universe) (Rev. 12:8-9) after Jesus resurrected and ascended to heaven.

Significance of Jobs' Hardships

When we are faced with tribulations and difficulties, we should not struggle to understand the impending hardships and tortures but the works of God hidden behind the tribulations. We must remember that no matter how strong and vehement the storms we encounter, bright sun light is always behind the storm, just as spring will come without fail after the coldest period of snowy winter. We must keep in mind that all our tribulations are controlled by Jehovah God the Creator who rules all things in the universe and directs our fate. As King David ran away from the revolt of his son Absalom, Shimei the son of Gera threw stones at him and cursed him (2 Sam. 16:5-11). "Then said Abishai the son of Zeruiah unto the king, Why should this dead dog curse my lord the king? Let me go over, I pray thee, and take off his head. And the king said, What have I to do with you, ye sons of Zeruiah? So let him curse, because the LORD hath said unto him, Curse David. Who shall then say, Wherefore hast thou done so?" (verses 9-10). David looked up to God, who takes care of his situations and conditions.

He wrote a Psalm that says, "I will not be afraid of ten thousands of people, that have set themselves against me round about" (Ps. 3:6,8).

Matthew 10:29 says, "Are not two sparrows sold for a farthing? And one of them shall not fall on the ground without your Father." This verse means nothing takes place unless God permits it. Any tribulations and adversities are an act of God's providence and will. Therefore, we must not only look at what is happening before our eyes but also look up to God, who takes care of and controls everything, and totally trust and rely on the Almighty God.

Benefits of Tribulations

As a misfortune turns into a blessing, so tribulations and hardships have benefits when we trust God. James 1:2 says, "My brethren, count it all joy when ye fall into divers temptations." "Blessed is the man that endureth temptation: for when he is tried, he shall receive the crown of life, which the Lord hath promised to them that love him" (Jam. 1:12). Hardships, tortures, and tribulations with which believers are faced are God's means and methods to provide us with His graces and advantages (Heb. 12:10; 1 Pet. 5:10). Therefore, we must not decide based on what is happening in front of us but look up to the hands of God the Father who manipulates everything happening to us. A way for us to avoid anxieties and worries is to focus our concern not on our anxieties and worries but on God's word, which encourages us.

After experiencing many tribulations, Job realizes that it is no more than a delusion for him to have known and trusted God in the past. After his hardships, he can correctly trust and believe in Jehovah God. Job 42:5-6 says, "I have heard of thee by the hearing of the ear: but now mine eye seeth thee.

Wherefore I abhor myself, and repent in dust and ashes." In addition, after his hardships, Job is doubly blessed and born again to receive God's grace. After tribulations and hardships, his misfortunes are turned into advantages as it is stated in Isaiah 1:25: "And I will turn my hand upon thee, and purely purge away thy dross, and take away all thy tin." Job confessed his positive faith in this manner, "But he knoweth the way that I take: when he hath tried me, I shall come forth as gold" (Job 23:10).

We may die suddenly without being blessed and be totally devastated to death. However, even in such a case, we will be benefited because we believe in, fear, and love God. Although we are evil, we love our children. How much more will God the Father love His children? We being selected as God's children should totally rely on and trust God the Father, in whose love and favor all things work together for good to us. Our tribulations may result from evil tricks of Satan (Job 2:3) or God's test (Gen. 22:1). Nevertheless, any tribulations may be a good opportunity for us to come closer to God, so we need not be fearful of such tribulations but give thanks to God.

Faith of a Child

A child tries to open a lock with a wrong key from a ring of keys. She tries for a long time to no avail. At last, she runs to her father and asks him to do for her. The father easily opens the door because he knows the right key to use. She believes that her father is an almighty one, who can always cake good care of her and do for her everything.

In Almighty God the Father, we must have such faith as this child she does. After experiencing hardships, Job came to have faith of a different dimension or faith of a born again Christian. He could totally trust and depend on Jehovah God.

Job was awakened afresh to God who loves him infinitely. He realized that current tribulations are never fruitless or evil but will definitely bring about a victorious life after being disciplined through torture. David says, "Before I was afflicted I went astray: but now have I kept thy word" (Ps. 119:67). And the Bible says, "And ye have forgotten the exhortation which speaketh unto you as unto children, My son, despise not thou the chastening of the Lord, nor faint when thou art rebuked of him" (Heb. 12:5-6).

"Blessed is the man that endureth temptation: for when he is tried, he shall receive the crown of life, which the Lord hath promised to them that love him" (Jam. 1:12). After being disciplined, Job realized that his faith had not been so good, and he repented of his arrogance in faith. We also must be warned against knowing God in an incorrect way and being arrogant of our faith. We must remove pride from our faith and be humble like a child and follow the footsteps of Christ Jesus toward our home country or heaven. In the name of Jesus Christ, I pray you the readers may be blessed and have faith like that of Esther, who said, "If I perish, I perish" (Es. 4:16).

APPENDIX 2

Prayers Answered

"And whatsoever ye shall ask in my name, that will I do, that the Father may be glorified in the Son. If ye shall ask any thing in my name, I will do it" (John 14:13-14).

Three major factors of our life of faith are: God's word, prayer, and obedience. Prayer is a means for us to communicate or converse with God. It is essential for a Christian life and should be learned at an initial step of the life. Why, then, are not all of the prayers answered? Why are many prayers seemingly not heard? It is because prayers are not made according to the teachings in the Bible. Below listed are the methods for prayers taught in the Bible.

1. Prayers in accordance with God's will

"And this is the confidence that we have in him, that, if we ask any thing according to his will, he heareth us" (1 John 5:14). "Ye ask, and receive not, because ye ask amiss, that ye may consume it upon your lusts" (James 4:3). Prayers will not be answered when they are made not in compliance with God's will but with our will. To set an example for us, Jesus made a prayer at the garden of Gethsemane and said, "Father, if thou be willing, remove this cup from me: nevertheless not my will, but thine, be done" (Luke 22:42).

First, we should present our prayers in accordance with God's will. God's will is to save all creation in this world, establish the everlasting heaven, and bring all the saved saints or God's selected ones who believe in Jesus Christ into the kingdom of heaven where they enjoy an everlasting life (John 6:40).

God's will also includes "your sanctification" (1 Thess. 4:3), which means that we are separated or consecrated through our believing in Jesus to be turned from children of darkness to children of light, from children of perdition to God's children. First Thessalonians 5:16-18 says, "Pray without ceasing. In everything give thanks: for this is the will of God in Christ Jesus concerning you." We should be always joyful in the Lord since we are enjoined, "Notwithstanding in this rejoice not, that the spirits are subject unto you; but rather rejoice, because your names are written in heaven" (Luke 10:20). When we realize the meaning of Romans 8:28, we can always rejoice in and pray to God, communicate, walk, and stay with Him and give Him thanks and praise for everything. Prayers made in accordance with God's will are centered on God and give the first priority to God.

2. Believing prayer

"And all things, whatsoever ye shall ask in prayer, believing, ye shall receive" (Matt. 21:22). You will receive answers whenever you ask in prayer, believing. Yet, your prayers may not be answered, for "But let him ask in faith, nothing wavering. For he that wavereth is like a wave of the sea driven with the wind and tossed" (Jam. 1:6-7). Your prayers will be answered when you ask in prayer, believing since Jesus says, "If thou canst believe, all things are possible to him that believeth" (Mark 9:23) and

"What things so ever ye desire, when ye pray, believe that ye receive them, and ye shall have them" (Mark 11:24). In Matthew 17:14-20, disciples asked to Jesus, "Why could not we cast him out?" Jesus answered, "Because of your unbelief." So the second key to prayers answered is belief.

3. Prayers earnestly made

"I say unto you, Though he will not rise and give him, because he is his friend, yet because of his importunity he will rise and give him as many as he needeth" (Luke 11:8). We must present our prayers earnestly and persistently. In the Bible, many times, a prayer is answered when it is made earnestly and persistently.

Luke 11:5-13 shows that a request is met not because the requester is a friend but because of his importunity. In Luke 18:1-8, a judge avenges a widow because of her importunate asking. Genesis 32:24-25 records a story of Jacob, who wrestled all night with God and at last was blessed from God. During the night when Jesus was arrested, he made a prayer at the garden of Gethsemane: "And being in an agony he prayed more earnestly: and his sweat was as it were great drops of blood falling down to the ground" (Luke 22:44). It is very hard but really essential that we should fervently present our prayer to God until it is answered. Sometimes, we must make a prayer at daybreak or at night, pray for one hundred days, make a fasting prayer, or all night prayer for a week or so until God answers it. Prayers answered are not necessarily ones made many times repeatedly or for a long time, because water cannot be boiled at a lower degrees than the tipping point even though it is heated for a prolonged period of time. A prayer, once made earnestly and sincerely and fervently enough, can be answered irrespective of the length of time in which it is made. A prayer made by a group of people or in a place of silence may be answered more easily. A prayer must be made persistently and ardently, which is not a piece of cake.

4. Prayers made in the name of Jesus Christ

"And whatsoever ye shall ask in my name, that will I do, that the Father may be glorified in the Son. If ye shall ask any thing in my name, I will do it" (John 14:13-14). Prayers will be answered when they are made in the Lord's name, since "whatsoever ye shall ask of the Father in my name, he may give it you" (John 15:16) and "whatsoever ye shall ask in my name, that will I do, that the Father may be glorified in the Son. If ye shall ask any thing in my name, I will do it" (John 14:13-14). "We pray in Jesus' name" must be always mentioned at the end of a prayer. Without this mentioning, prayer cannot be presented to the throne of God and answered, although it is made persistently and fervently. Because "Jesus saith unto him, I am the way, the truth, and the life: no man cometh unto the Father, but by me" (John 14:6).

Our Lord's name is Jesus (Matt. 1:21; Luke 1:31, 2:21), Christ (Matt. 16:16; Mark 8:29; Luke 9:20; John 4:26) or Immanuel (Isa. 7:14; Matt. 1:23). Jesus is the Lord's personal name while Christ (John 1:41) is His public name or title, as is confessed by Peter (Matt. 16:16). In the Bible, several people have Jesus as their personal name (Luke 3:29; Acts 13:6; Col. 4:11). So, Jesus Christ is a correct and proper name of our Lord. Alternatives are Jesus Christ of Nazareth (Acts 3:6, 4:10), habitually used by Peter, and Jesus Christ, favored by Paul. In order to get our prayers answered, we should not forget to mention the name of Jesus Christ, which is sometimes omitted, at the end of our prayer.

Lastly, let me say something about the Lord's Prayer (Matt. 6:9-13), which is taught by Jesus Himself. It is composed of seven sentences: three refer to the kingdom of heaven and God, and four refer to His children, with the ending for praising God. In this prayer, one sentence asks for daily bread and a request is made not to overcome temptation but to not be led into temptation. Our sin may hinder our prayer from being answered, according to Mark 11:25. Our prayers can be communicated to God freely when we forgive so that our Father may forgive our sins.

I pray that your fervent prayers will be answered in the name of Jesus, and that our Lord's remarkable grace and peace may be with you until you win the crown of victory!

APPENDIX 3

A History of the Bible

Here is a brief history of the Bible. The Old Testament is composed of thirty-nine books written in Hebrew by thirty-two writers between about 1450 BC and about 400 BC, a period of about 1,100 years. Four passages were written in the Aramaic language: Ezra 4:8-6:18 and 7:12-26; Jeremiah 10:11; and Daniel 2:4 and 7:28.

The Hebrew Old Testament was translated into Greek by order of Ptolemy , an Egyptian king (283-247 BC). The translation, called the Septuagint (or LXX) was completed around 277 by seventy-two Jews—six from each of the twelve Jewish tribes. About the second century AD, the Targum (Ezra 4:7) translation of the Old Testament was produced in Aramaic, which was a contemporary language of Jews.

Between 600 and about 940 AD, Jewish masorah scholars produced the so-called new masoretic (*massora* means "tradition") text of Old Testament. In this text, twenty-three Hebrew consonants were added with twenty vowel marks (∵, T, :, -, etc.) and accents, so as to make the text more readable and understandable. Ancient Hebrew did not have vowels; the masorah scholars created them in the sixth and seventh centuries, so the marks are also called masoretic vowel marks.

The New Testament was written in Greek (except for some passages in Aramaic) by at least eight writers (the writer of the book Hebrews is unknown) over a period of seventy years. So, both New and Old Testaments were written by about forty writers who were inspired by God (2 Tim. 3:16). Origen of Alexandria (184-254 AD) compiled hexapla, the New Testament edited in six languages. Roman Emperor Constantine (280-337), who converted to Christianity in 312 AD, issued Milan Edict in 315 to officially recognize the religion and gave an order to do no work on Sundays in 321. He ordered fifty copies of the Bible in Greek.

Obeying this command, Eusebius the Bishop of Caesarea, produced the manuscripts in 331. Of the these, only two are extant: Codex Vaticanus and Codex Sinaiticus. Codex Vaticanus was found in 1475 from the Vatican library and is kept in the papal court. Codex Sinaiticus was found in 1859 by Lobegott Friedrich Constantin Tischendorf (1815-1874), a German Biblical scholar from St. Catherine's Abbey at the foot of Mt. Sinai. Under the auspices of Russian Emperor Leipzig, the codex was published in four books, including the apocrypha and the pseudograph in 1862. It is now in the British Museum.

Pope Damasus ordered Jerome (340-420) to produce a Latin Bible, which would be officially used in the papal court. The Latin version produced by Jerome is called the Vulgate, of which New Testament was completed around 388 and the Old Testament around 415. Codex Alexandrianus, which is a Greek version known to have been produced in the early fifth century, was found in 1627 with parts of its Old Testament and New Testament missing. It has been kept in the British Museum since then. The Codex Leningrad, written in 1008, is one of the extant oldest codices. In the Middle Ages, between the fifth and fifteenth centuries, the Bible was translated into about thirty-three languages. It was translated in ancient English around the seventh century, and the whole Bible was translated in medieval English in the fourteenth century by John Wycliffe (1321-1384), an English theologian. In 1611, the King James Version was produced.

In the Far East, the Bible was translated into Chinese by Robert Morrison, a missionary to China, in 1823, and the New Testament was translated into Japanese by missionary S. R. Brown in 1879. The New Testament was translated into Korean by John Ross in 1887 and the Old Testament in 1920. In 1937, a revised version was produced in Korean.

The Qumran scrolls, or the Dead Sea scrolls, were found in 1947 in caves along the northwest shore of the Dead Sea, which is known to have been a stronghold of the Essenes. For nine years, between 1947 and 1956, about nine hundred scriptural fragments were found in eleven caves. Naturally, the Hebrew parchment scrolls do not have New Testament texts. They comprise all the Old Testament books, including the apocrypha, except for parts of Esther and Nehemiah, and were produced between about 200 BC and AD 70.

In AD 381, Roman Emperor Theodosius I (346-395) completely excluded from the empire religions other than Christianity and officially proclaimed the canons of New and Old Testaments. In 397, the Carthage synods in North Africa decided thirty-nine books of the Old Testament and twenty-seven books of New Testament as they are today.

The New Testament was written on papyrus till about the seventh century or on sheepskin and cowhide after that time. The Bible books were produced in scrolls in ancient times but later they were gradually published in the form of codex. Greek majuscule manuscripts were produced before about the eighth century and minuscule manuscripts after that. Most of

New Testament manuscripts are in codex. The manuscripts are counted according to their certification number, which comes to more than 10,000 in Latin documents and more than 7,500 in Greek. Some manuscripts are not so big as a palm and contain only several Bible verses.

All the ancient Bible books were manuscripts. The first printed Bible, which does not divide chapters and verses, was printed in Latin in 1456. In 1228, Stephen Langton (1150-1228) first divided the Bible into chapters (the whole Bible contains 1,189 chapters). The Bible was first divided into verses in 1448 by R. Nathan, and in 1551 AD by Robert Stephanus (1503-1559). The Geneva Bible, published in 1560, is the first to print the chapters and verses.

Today, the Protestant Bible contains sixty-six books—thirty -nine in the Old Testament and twenty-seven in the New Testament—1,189 chapters, including 929 chapters in Old Testament and 260 ones in New Testament, and 31,173 verses, including 23,214 Old Testament verses and 7,959 New Testament verses.

The first printed Greek New Testament was produced by Desiderius Erasmus (1469-1536) in 1516. In 1531 when the second printed Greek edition was published, the Bible was distorted. That is, such verses as 1 John 5:7 were added to the first edition (see *Misquoting Jesus*, by Bart Ehrman). In the Korean revised version, this verse reads: "And it is the Spirit that bears witness, because the Spirit is truth" instead of "For there are three that bear record in heaven, the Father, the Word, and the Holy Ghost: and these three are one," as is in the King James Version, which was published in 1611 and follows the Textus Receptus, the second printed Greek edition considered the Greek standard original text. The Textus Receptus was changed so that verse 7 is merged with verse 6 and then verse

7 is newly invented and added. No ancient authoritative Greek manuscripts of New Testament a new verse 7, except for some Latin translations written before the 16th century, which carry the verse in question, since it may be that anyone who denied the trinity or acted against the popes could be punished. Since then, all arguments about the trinity has been taboo and considered heresy. The King James Version revised and published recently does not have the controversial verse 7.

Another example of the distortion of the Bible is 1 Timothy 3:16, which reads, "He was manifest in the flesh" (the Korean revised version) instead of "God was manifest in the flesh" (KJV). This distortion was attributed to that fact that He (Ος in Greek, pointing to Jesus) was intentionally supplanted with God (Θς in Greek) in the original language of the verse. Traditional texts like Codex Vaticanus and Codex Sinaiticus do not have such confusion, which was found and proved by Johan J. Wettstein (1693-1754) who was a Protestant and allowed to personally investigate the Codex Alexandrianus, which is kept in the British Museum.

A warning is given to priests in Malachi 1:6-8: "A son honoureth his father, and a servant his master: if then I be a father, where is mine honour? and if I be a master, where is my fear? saith the LORD of hosts unto you, O priests, that despise my name. And ye say, Wherein have we despised thy name? Ye offer polluted bread upon mine altar; and ye say, Wherein have we polluted thee? In that ye say, The table of the LORD is contemptible. And if ye offer the blind for sacrifice, is it not evil? and if ye offer the lame and sick, is it not evil? offer it now unto thy governor; will he be pleased with thee, or accept thy person? saith the LORD of hosts."

I know a man who told me about a dream he had. While people are being judged in front of God's white throne, God asks the man, "Why did you say what the Bible says nothing about?" He replies, "The Bible says nothing, but renowned theologians and pastors said so. I just followed their footsteps." "Oh," says God. "You need to look over there." Over there, many people were falling off the end of a cliff and crying aloud, as is stated in the Bible, "Enter ye in at the strait gate: for wide is the gate, and broad is the way, that leadeth to destruction, and many there be which go in thereat" (Matt. 7:13).

There are four English terms to denote perpetuity (αιων in Greek and נצח in Hebrew) without beginning or end: forever, everlasting, eternal, and permanence. *Permanence* means unchangeable perpetuity, while *forever* and *everlasting* mean perpetuity from the present, and *eternal* means perpetuity from the past. God the Father is self-existing in eternity, having neither beginning nor end like a circle.